MARGARET FEINBERG

THE GOD YOU NEED TO KNOW

12 PRACTICES TO AWAKEN YOUR RELATIONSHIP WITH THE HOLY SPIRIT

The God You Need to Know Bible Study Guide
© 2025 by Margaret Feinberg

Published in Grand Rapids, Michigan, by HarperChristian Resources, 3950 Sparks Drive SE, Suite 101, Grand Rapids, MI 49546, USA. HarperChristian Resources is a registered trademark of HarperCollins Christian Publishing, Inc.

Requests for information should be sent to customercare@harpercollins.com.

ISBN 978-0-310-13122-9 (softcover)
ISBN 978-0-310-13123-6 (ebook)

All Scripture quotations unless otherwise noted are taken from the Holy Bible, New International Version®, NIV®. Copyright © 1973, 1978, 1984, 2011 by Biblica, Inc.® Used by permission. All rights reserved worldwide.

Scripture quotations marked ESV are taken from the ESV® Bible (The Holy Bible, English Standard Version®). Copyright © 2001 by Crossway, a publishing ministry of Good News Publishers. Used by permission. All rights reserved.

Scripture quotations marked MSG are taken from *The Message*. Copyright © by Eugene H. Peterson 1993, 1994, 1995, 1996, 2000, 2001, 2002. Used by permission of NavPress. All rights reserved. Represented by Tyndale House Publishers, Inc.

Scripture quotations marked CSB are taken from the Christian Standard Bible®, Copyright © 2017 by Holman Bible Publishers. Used by permission. Christian Standard Bible®, and CSB®, are federally registered trademarks of Holman Bible Publishers.

Any internet addresses (websites, blogs, etc.) and telephone numbers in this study guide are offered as a resource. They are not intended in any way to be or imply an endorsement by HarperChristian Resources, nor does HarperChristian Resources vouch for the content of these sites and numbers for the life of this study guide.

All rights reserved. No portion of this book may be reproduced, stored in a retrieval system, or transmitted in any form or by any means—electronic, mechanical, photocopy, recording, scanning, or other—except for brief quotations in critical reviews or articles, without the prior written permission of the publisher.

HarperChristian Resources titles may be purchased in bulk for church, business, fundraising, or ministry use. For information, please email ResourceSpecialist@ChurchSource.com.

Author is represented by The Christopher Ferebee Agency, www.christopherferebee.com.

Without limiting the exclusive rights of any author, contributor or the publisher of this publication, any unauthorized use of this publication to train generative artificial intelligence (AI) technologies is expressly prohibited. HarperCollins also exercise their rights under Article 4(3) of the Digital Single Market Directive 2019/790 and expressly reserve this publication from the text and data mining exception.

HarperCollins Publishers, Macken House, 39/40 Mayor Street Upper, Dublin 1, D01 C9W8, Ireland
(https://www.harpercollins.com)

Art Direction: Ron Huizinga
Cover Design: Susie Nelson of Willow and Sage Floral Design, Benjamin Haupt, and Margaret Feinberg
Interior Design: Lauren Rives

First Printing June 2025 / Printed in the United States of America

CONTENTS

Invitation from Margaret 4

How to Use This Study Guide 6

SESSION 1 | In Step with the Spirit 11

SESSION 2 | The Spirit Who Hovers 49

SESSION 3 | The Spirit Who Makes 91

SESSION 4 | The Beauty of Discernment 127

SESSION 5 | The Spirit's Delightful Surprises 171

SESSION 6 | When the Spirit Says "Go!" 201

Leader's Guide 230

Meet Margaret 247

INVITATION FROM MARGARET

Hi, friend.

I'll confess that I've struggled to know and recognize the Holy Spirit in my life and in my community. I loved reading Jesus stories throughout the Gospels as a kid. Through their depiction of Christ's humanity, I could picture his compassionate eyes and hearty laughter. And from biblical descriptions of God the Father, I grew comfortable with the image of God on his throne—sovereign and powerful.

But when it came to the Holy Spirit, I struggled to wrap my head and heart around the one who Jesus once compared to the wind: "The wind blows wherever it pleases. You hear its sound, but you cannot tell where it comes from or where it is going" (John 3:8). Unseen but undeniably moving.

Maybe you can relate. Perhaps you've heard about the Holy Spirit in sermons or read about the Spirit in Scripture but still feel like the Spirit is an unfamiliar notion rather than a living presence in your life—more like a theological concept than a divine companion.

Now when it comes to the Holy Spirit, I'm far from an expert. I'm just a fellow learner on this journey of following God. But I've recently discovered the Holy Spirit anew by examining the Spirit's presence throughout the Old Testament. What I've learned has helped me love the Spirit of the Living God even more, and I hope it will for you too.

I remember curling up in my couch one morning, the pages of Exodus resting in front of me, when I felt it—that gentle stirring, like the rustling of leaves before the rain. The ancient words about the Spirit suddenly felt as fresh as the morning dew, and I realized I had been looking for something complex while the Spirit of God had been breathing beside me all along.

Together through this study, we're going to discover how the Holy Spirit is not merely a force or an idea—the Spirit is the very presence of God, hovering over chaos, residing within us, guiding us, empowering us, and transforming us from the inside out. The Spirit is the breath of God who gives us life, the whisper in the storm that Elijah heard, and the Comforter who never abandons us.

The God You Need to Know is an invitation not to theological debates or abstract discussions but rather to an intimate relationship with the Holy Spirit, filling our lives with power and peace that surpasses understanding.

As you turn these pages, my prayer is that you will encounter the Holy Spirit afresh through deep biblical study and simple practices that empower you to walk in step with the Spirit. Whether you are new to the idea of faith or have journeyed with God for years, the Holy Spirit has more for you—more wonder, more comfort, more power, more love.

Are you ready to embark on a journey that will forever change the way you see and experience God? If so, take a deep breath—the Spirit is already here, waiting to meet you in these pages, in this moment, in your very breath.

With all my love,

♡ Margaret ♡

HOW TO USE THIS STUDY GUIDE

GROUP SIZE AND RECOMMENDATIONS

The God You Need to Know video study is designed to be experienced in a group setting such as a Bible study, Sunday school class, or small group gathering. To facilitate meaningful discussion among larger groups, divide participants in groups of four to six following the teaching video. Select one person in each group to act as the facilitator during the discussion time. Of course, you can always work through the material and watch the videos on your own if a group is unavailable. But this study, in particular, is designed to be experienced with others. Consider calling a few friends or neighbors to join in the fun.

MATERIALS NEEDED

To gain the most from this study, each participant should have their own copy of this study guide as well as their own copy of the book *The God You Need to Know*. Each study guide comes with individual streaming video access to the six teaching videos. Every member of your group has full access to watch videos from the convenience of their chosen devices at any time—for missed group meetings, for rewatching, or for sharing the teaching with others. This gives your group the flexibility to make the experience doable no matter your unique circumstances.

LEADING A GROUP

Each group should appoint a leader or facilitator who is responsible for starting the video and keeping track of time during the activities and discussion.

Facilitators may also read questions aloud, monitor discussions, prompt participants to respond, and ensure that everyone has the opportunity to participate.

You do not need to buy the book to complete this Bible study. However, for the most comprehensive experience, it's recommended to read the suggested chapters as you go through the study.

There's a Leader's Guide in the back of each study guide so anyone can lead a group through this study.

WEEKLY SCHEDULE

There are a variety of ways to experience this study:
1. Meet, watch the videos, and discuss the questions.
2. Meet, watch the videos, discuss the questions, and do the homework.
3. Meet, watch the videos, discuss the questions, do the homework, and read the book.

Select the option that best fits your group and time restraints. Groups who choose option 3 often extend the time to go through the content at a slower place.

This study guide includes group activities, video outline notes, group discussion questions, personal study days for between group meetings, and Scripture memory coloring pages to deepen learning between sessions.

At the beginning of each session, the study guide suggests chapters of the book to read before the next gathering. Each personal study day will lead participants deeper into the scriptural content of the video or book. On the next page, you'll find a sample of the schedule that appears at the beginning of every new week.

OPTIONAL BEFORE GROUP MEETING	Read chapters _____ in *The God You Need to Know* book.
DURING GROUP MEETING	Watch teaching video for Session _____. Group discussion will follow, pages _____.
PERSONAL STUDY DAY 1	Study guide pages _____
PERSONAL STUDY DAY 2	Study guide pages _____
PERSONAL STUDY DAY 3	Study guide pages _____
PERSONAL STUDY CATCH-UP DAYS 4 & 5	Complete any unfinished Personal Study activities. Optional: Read chapters _____ in *The God You Need to Know* book.

TIMING

The timing notations—for example, twenty minutes—indicate the actual length of the video segments and the suggested times for each activity or discussion. Within your allotted group meeting time, you may not get to all the discussion questions. Remember that the quantity of questions addressed isn't as important as the quality of the discussion.

Your group may choose to use a single session for two meetings rather than one. This option allows conversations to explore more fully the content of the study guide and the book. While the first meeting could be devoted to watching the teaching video and responding to the group questions, the second meeting could be devoted to exploring the insights gained from the personal study days.

Using the Leader's Guide in the back of the guide to review the content overview of each session and the group discussion questions in advance will give you a good idea of which questions you want to focus on as a leader or group facilitator.

OPENING GROUP DISCUSSION AND ACTIVITY

Depending on the amount of time you meet and the resources available, you'll find discussion questions at the beginning of every lesson and optional activities at the beginning of Sessions 3 and 6. These interactive questions and activities are designed to be a catalyst for group engagement and help participants prepare and transition to the ideas explored in the video teaching.

The leader or facilitator will want to read ahead to the following week's activity to see what will be needed and how participants may be able to contribute by bringing supplies or refreshments.

"Pentecost unfolds with a regalia of signs and wonders and unity and generosity that become markers of the early church. No wonder we still turn to the second chapter of Acts to see this work of the Spirit. Yet this is *not* the Spirit's grand debut; it's a culmination of centuries of the Spirit's work throughout the world."

FROM *THE GOD YOU NEED TO KNOW*
p. 11

SESSION ONE

IN STEP WITH THE SPIRIT

GROUP STUDY

SCHEDULE

OPTIONAL BEFORE GROUP MEETING	Pick up a copy of *The God You Need to Know* book.
DURING GROUP MEETING	Watch teaching video for Session 1. Group discussion will follow, pages 16–21.
PERSONAL STUDY DAY 1	Study guide pages 23–29
PERSONAL STUDY DAY 2	Study guide pages 30–39
PERSONAL STUDY DAY 3	Study guide pages 40–45
PERSONAL STUDY CATCH-UP DAYS 4 & 5	Complete any unfinished Personal Study activities. Optional: Read chapters 1–2 in *The God You Need to Know* book.

 5–10 minutes

OPENING GROUP DISCUSSION

In upcoming Sessions 3 and 6, we'll have group activities, but for this opening session we'll begin with some discussion questions. Since everyone joins with different reasons, goals, and hopes, please:

Introduce yourself briefly (if this is your group's first meeting).

Share your response to at least one of the following questions:

What motivated you to join this study group?

What's one hope you have for this study—something you want to learn, experience, or explore?

BONUS

Take a photo of your group and send it to hello@margaretfeinberg.com. Our team would love to see your smiling faces and pray for your group.

 26 minutes

SESSION 1 VIDEO

Leader, stream the video or play the DVD.

> **SCRIPTURE COVERED IN THIS TEACHING SESSION:**
> Genesis 1:2;
> Psalm 51:10–11;
> Judges 15:14;
> Acts 2:1–18

VIDEO NOTES

As you watch, use the outline to help you follow along and take notes on anything that stands out to you.

Story of the "air comforter"—*This is new, different, and I'm comfortable where I am.*

Perichoresis describes the internal relationship of the members of the Trinity.

Peri meaning "around" + *choresis* meaning "dance" = choreography

Jesus gives his disciples a parting gift they'll treasure forever.

Paraclete means Advocate, Helper, Counselor, Comforter, and Strengthener.

The Holy Spirit is all over the Old Testament.

Acts 2—*Of course, it would happen this way!*

Marinate in Scripture.

Make space to listen.

Talk about the Holy Spirit with others.

 30–45 minutes

GROUP DISCUSSION QUESTIONS

Leader note: *Take a few moments to review these questions, then feel free to add some of your own or whisk away any that aren't a good fit for your group. Remember, our goal isn't to cover every question but to foster meaningful discussion and experience those heart-to-heart moments that draw us closer to each other and to God as we journey together—trusting the Spirit to guide our conversations.*

What challenged, encouraged, or stood out to you about this first session?

1. I tell the story of the "air comforter" to illustrate that we all have moments in our spiritual lives where we think, *This is different. I'm comfortable where I am. You can just keep that over there.* And later, we discover this is the greatest gift ever.

    When you hear the phrase "Holy Spirit," what's the first image, feeling, or thought that comes to mind?

    What's one experience or teaching that shaped your understanding (or confusion) about the Holy Spirit?

2. The internal relationship of the Trinity is described using the word *perichoresis*, meaning "choreography." Whenever God moves, all the members of the Trinity work together in a dance of mutual admiration, love, and mission, delighting in one another. In this beautiful dance, one member of the Trinity may take the lead, but the others always are in step.

    What are some of the ways you've heard the Trinity described to you?

    Which have been most helpful?

    What comes to mind when you imagine the Trinity in a dance?

3. Invite volunteers to read the following scriptures aloud to the group: Genesis 1:2, Psalm 51:10–11, and Judges 15:14. After each passage is read, pause to answer the following questions:

    How is the Holy Spirit described or what role is the Spirit playing in this passage?

    How does this Old Testament view of the Spirit compare to anything you've understood about the Holy Spirit from the New Testament?

In what ways might these passages challenge or expand your current understanding of the Holy Spirit's work?

4. In this study, we look at Acts 2:1–18 in both this first session and in the final session. As a group, let's take a few moments to reflect on Pentecost. Ask participants to take turns reading through Acts 2:1–18 aloud. Then, invite each person to jot down notes regarding the following questions. After making some personal notes, discuss your answers.

    How do you think the disciples felt before the Holy Spirit entered this way compared to after? Can you relate to either of these states in your own spiritual journey? If so, describe.

    In what ways has the Holy Spirit worked as a unifying force in your life, bringing people together despite their differences (like language in this passage)?

    What's one way you'd love to experience the Spirit working in your own life, maybe like the believers in Acts 2?

5. I encourage us to "marinate in scripture." I shared two examples. Once, a student quietly passed me a note containing Isaiah 43 during a difficult time. Another comes from Elenna, who found unexpected strength in Isaiah 41:10 after her husband's sudden death.

   What's one Scripture that has come alive for you in a fresh way because of the Spirit?

   What was happening in your life at the time?

   Where in your life do you sense God's presence has been quietly holding you, even if you didn't notice it at first?

   How would you describe your relationship with the Holy Spirit today, and how do you hope it will grow through this study?

   How has listening to others share their experiences with the Holy Spirit in the group today changed or expanded your own understanding?

   How might our community grow if we became more comfortable discussing the Holy Spirit's activity in our lives?

BEFORE THE NEXT SESSION...

Every week, this study guide includes five days of personal study to help awaken your relationship with the Holy Spirit through Scripture.

- Tackle the three days of personal study (with two days to catch up and reflect) for Session 1.

- Optional: Read chapters 1–2 of *The God You Need to Know* book.

- Memorize this week's passage using the Scripture memory coloring page. As a bonus, look up the Scripture memory passage in different translations and take note of the variations.

- Try the three practices from this session and be prepared to share how it went at the next gathering.

CLOSE IN PRAYER

Consider the following prompts as you pray together for:

- Increasing awareness and attentiveness to the Spirit

- Scripture to spark life in fresh and meaning ways

- Prompts and nudges to share Christ's love

If you then, though you are evil, know how to give good gifts to your children, how much more will your Father in heaven give the Holy Spirit to those who ask him! Luke 11:13

SESSION ONE

IN STEP WITH THE SPIRIT

PERSONAL STUDY

PERSONAL STUDY DAY 1

HOLY SPIRIT, WHO ARE YOU?

Years ago, my friend Marcus saved up to take his family on vacation—a rare treat for his three children and his beloved wife. When they arrived at the hotel, a staff member materialized beside the front desk.

"Can I offer any of you a refreshing drink?" the staff member asked.

Dollar signs spun like a game-show wheel in Marcus's mind. The family was on a tight budget, each expense calculated with the precision of an anxious mathematician.

"Thank you, but we're good," he announced, his voice a thin disguise for worry.

After checking in, his wife pulled a diet soda from the mini-bar and popped it open with a satisfying hiss. Marcus lunged for a printed menu, then reminded her about the legendary costs of in-room snacks before hurrying to ensure his children hadn't discovered the snacks in their room.

As the family headed to the beach, a staff member appeared, arms filled with clean, warm towels.

"You'll need these," she offered.

"Are you sure?" Marcus asked, hands hesitating midair, seeing each towel marked with invisible price tags. He gingerly accepted the towels, and the staff member vanished before he could properly thank her.

Later, returning sun-soaked from the beach, another employee offered, "Can I make you a dinner reservation at our restaurant tonight?"

Marcus imagined the size of a sit-down restaurant bill. "We're good, but thank you," he said, already mentally mapping the route to the nearest fast-food establishment.

That evening, the family slipped away to an inexpensive restaurant, sharing French fries and drinking water to save precious resources. This pattern continued throughout their stay—eating at budget restaurants beyond the hotel grounds, gathering provisions from a local grocery store like wilderness survivors.

Meanwhile, Marcus and his family basked in the hotel's unexpected generosities: the attentive staff who materialized with fresh towels before beach excursions, umbrellas that appeared precisely when rain began to fall, and bottles of water that the staff assured Marcus—each time with increasing emphasis—were "complimentary."

When the time came for checkout, Marcus approached the front desk with the hidden confidence that he'd beat the system. Other than his wife's single diet soda, he'd managed to avoid any additional charges. But when the hotel clerk presented his bill, even that small indulgence had been erased.

Marcus felt a twinge of honesty nudge him. "I think you're missing a charge for a soda from our room's refrigerator," he said.

"Sir, those are complimentary," the clerk responded.

"What?" he asked. "I don't understand."

"This is an all-inclusive resort, sir," the clerk explained. "Everything—meals, drinks, activities, and service—it's all included in the price you paid when you booked."

Marcus still shakes his head in disbelief when he retells his vacation story—everything was all-included, but he spent the entire time living as if it weren't.

He accepted a few small provisions but declined the grand feasts.

Sometimes when I think about Marcus's story, I can't help but see it as a parable for our spiritual lives. Many of us live as visitors in an all-inclusive kingdom, clutching our resources tightly, declining God's extravagant offerings, living on spiritual fast food when a banquet table has been prepared.

All-included in our relationship with God through Jesus is the Holy Spirit.

Who is the Holy Spirit?

The Spirit is not an optional upgrade or premium feature but an essential presence that transforms our spiritual experience from austere to abundant. The Spirit stands attentive, eager to offer strength where we're depleted, to lift burdens we were never designed to carry alone, and to illuminate paths that would otherwise remain obscure.

Sure, you can attempt this journey on your own strength. But why would you? That would be like going to an all-inclusive resort and insisting on paying for everything separately when it has already been provided, already been paid for, already been included.

The question is not whether the Holy Spirit is available to you—the question is whether you'll accept, experience, and enjoy what, or rather who, you've already been given.

When have you found yourself, like Marcus, declining something freely offered because you couldn't believe it was really included?

Read Acts 2:38. How is the Holy Spirit described?

How might this change how you think about and approach a relationship with the Holy Spirit?

Marcus missed out on many amenities because he didn't understand what was included. What aspects of the Holy Spirit's presence and power might you be overlooking or declining in your daily life?

Read John 14:16. What does Jesus reveal about the Holy Spirit in this verse?

In the story about Marcus's vacation, the hotel staff kept appearing at just the right moments with just what was needed.

Have you ever experienced a moment of unexpected help, guidance, or comfort that came just when you needed it? Whether you recognized it as the Holy Spirit at the time or not, what was that experience like for you?

What did it reveal to you about the character, competence, or kindness of God?

Read Romans 8:26. Reflect on a specific time when God's strength sustained you beyond what you thought possible. What did that reveal about the Spirit's work in your life?

> "If you then, though you are evil, know how to give good gifts to your children, how much more will your Father in heaven give the Holy Spirit to those who ask him!"
>
> Luke 11:13

Reflecting on Luke 11:13 above, what would you like to ask of the Holy Spirit today?

Marcus eventually learned the truth about his all-inclusive package, but this didn't occur until the end of his stay.

What daily practice might help you stay aware of the Spirit's presence and provisions?

The Holy Spirit isn't waiting for you to earn special access or save up spiritual currency. You don't need to anxiously check the price list before accepting what God freely offers. The Spirit—with all gifts, fruit, and power—is already included in what Jesus purchased for you. The question isn't, "Can I afford this?" but rather, "How might my life transform as I embrace what's already freely given?"

PERSONAL STUDY DAY 2

HOLY SPIRIT, I THINK I WANT TO KNOW YOU

There is a guest who has been moving through the rooms of your life since before you had words to name what you needed. Sometimes, in rare moments of clarity—perhaps during a sunset that shatters your defenses or in the warm silence after a friend's embrace—you catch a glimpse of this presence. Not with your eyes, exactly, but with something deeper, like the way you internally know when someone has entered a room even before you turn around.

This is the Spirit who hovered over the waters, the wind that parts seas, and the fire that doesn't consume. And yet, for all this cosmic drama, the Spirit often comes to us in sacred echoes, in gentle nudges, in questions that arrive unexpectedly at three in the morning.

When we say, "Holy Spirit, I think I want to know you," we may be tempted to approach the Spirit cautiously, the way you might approach a deer in a forest clearing—aware that any sudden movement on our part might send this wild thing disappearing into the trees. Yet the Spirit isn't shy, as some claim; the Spirit is willing and ready.

Just like any vibrant relationship, a relationship with the Spirit can't be forced or scripted or reduced into formulaic, rote prayers. Rather, a relationship with the Spirit is built over time, nurtured, and attended to—just as you would a dear friend.

Take a moment and prayerfully imagine introducing yourself to the Holy Spirit. Sure, the Spirit already knows you inside and out.

Now, as you continue the conversation, what questions would you ask the Spirit? They can be on anything that naturally comes to mind. (Examples: *Where are you from? What do you like to do? What brings you joy?*)

This simple practice of introducing ourselves to the Spirit and prayerfully engaging in a natural conversation may be new to you, but something shifts in us when we become more attentive to the nearness of the Holy Spirit. Like discovering that the stranger who has been helping you gather dropped papers on a windy day is the author of your favorite book, you're in for a beautiful surprise when you look up.

What might change in you as you increasingly acknowledge the one who has been waiting for you to notice all along?

We sometimes mistakenly view the Holy Spirit as lesser in importance simply because of the familiar ordering we encounter creeds: "Father, Son, and Spirit." This common sequence can unconsciously lead us to apply human rankings where none exist.

Within the Trinity, there's no hierarchy or ranking—no first, second, or third in significance. Each person of the Trinity—Father, Son, and Spirit—exists in perfect equality and unity, sharing fully in the divine nature and purpose.

The Holy Spirit is fully God. This means the Spirit possesses all the divine attributes of God the Father and God the Son. The Spirit is not a representative of God or an agent of God but is equally God, co-eternal with the Father and the Son. This foundational truth helps us delight in who the Spirit is and the vital relationship the Spirit desires with us.

Let's discover together what that might look like. The character, personality, and presence of the Holy Spirit is revealed throughout Scripture. So if we want to become more attentive to the presence and prompts of the Spirit, then the practices of **Marinating in Scripture** and **Making Space to Listen** are essential.

Let's embark on an adventure with the Holy Spirit—whether you're old friends or just getting acquainted.

Over the next few pages you'll find passages that offer glimpses into how the Spirit works in our lives. Instead of rushing through, let's try something a little different.

1. **Take a breath and slow down.** This isn't a race! Read each Scripture passage as if you're savoring a delicious meal rather than grabbing fast food.

2. **Get curious.** You might want to underline or circle words that jump out at you (like finding hidden treasures in plain sight).

3. **Listen with your heart.** Sometimes the most important conversations happen in quiet moments. These prompts are for you to ask, listen, and record whatever you might hear.

PASSAGE 1

But if Christ is in you, then even though your body is subject to death because of sin, the Spirit gives life because of righteousness. And if the Spirit of him who raised Jesus from the dead is living in you, he who raised Christ from the dead will also give life to your mortal bodies because of his Spirit who lives in you.
Romans 8:10–11

Holy Spirit, what does this passage teach me about you?

Holy Spirit, what does this passage reveal to me about your presence and work in my life now?

Holy Spirit, is there an invitation here for me? Something I'm being nudged toward?

PASSAGE 2

For those who are led by the Spirit of God are the children of God. The Spirit you received does not make you slaves, so that you live in fear again; rather, the Spirit you received brought about your adoption to sonship. And by him we cry, "Abba, Father." The Spirit himself testifies with our spirit that we are God's children.
Romans 8:14–16

Holy Spirit, what does this passage teach me about you?

Holy Spirit, what does this passage reveal to me about your presence and work in my life now?

Holy Spirit, is there an invitation here for me? Something I'm being nudged toward?

PASSAGE 3

And we all, who with unveiled faces contemplate the Lord's glory, are being transformed into his image with ever-increasing glory, which comes from the Lord, who is the Spirit.
2 Corinthians 3:18

Holy Spirit, what does this passage teach me about you?

Holy Spirit, what does this passage reveal to me about your presence and work in my life now?

Holy Spirit, is there an invitation here for me? Something I'm being nudged toward?

PASSAGE 4

> . . . because our gospel came to you not simply with words but also with power, with the Holy Spirit and deep conviction.
> 1 Thessalonians 1:5

Holy Spirit, what does this passage teach me about you?

Holy Spirit, what does this passage reveal to me about your presence and work in my life now?

Holy Spirit, is there an invitation here for me? Something I'm being nudged toward?

PASSAGE 5

> But you, dear friends, by building yourselves up in your most holy faith and praying in the Holy Spirit, keep yourselves in God's love as you wait for the mercy of our Lord Jesus Christ to bring you to eternal life.
>
> Jude 1:20–21

Holy Spirit, what does this passage teach me about you?

Holy Spirit, what does this passage reveal to me about your presence and work in my life now?

Holy Spirit, is there an invitation here for me? Something I'm being nudged toward?

When you open Scripture, you're never sitting there alone with just ink and paper or a screen. The Spirit is like that enthusiastic friend who says, "Oh! Remember that part Jesus talked about? Let me show you how that fits perfectly into what you're facing today." That's the Holy Spirit—eagerly waiting to turn the words from the Bible's pages into vibrant, life-giving invitations to transformation.

Let's take a few minutes to get to know the Holy Spirit a little more. Look up the passages listed and fill in the chart.

Bible Passage	How does this passage encourage you about the Holy Spirit's presence and work in your life?
John 16:13–15	
Acts 1:8	
1 Corinthians 2:13	
1 Corinthians 3:16	
2 Corinthians 3:18	

Remember, the Spirit is like that surprise gift you didn't know you needed until you unwrapped it. The Spirit is with you like a friend who knows all your secrets yet stays anyway, a guide who sees the entire map when you're lost in the undergrowth, a power source when your own batteries have long gone flat, and a translator who understands your wordless groans and turns them into perfect prayer.

What extravagant generosity that the very breath of God would choose to make a home in you!

PERSONAL STUDY DAY 3

HOLY SPIRIT, I'D LIKE TO KNOW MORE ABOUT YOU

The Holy Spirit dances into our lives like an unexpected gift—the kind wrapped in shimmering paper that makes you catch your breath when you discover it. Now, if we're going to *know* more about the Spirit, that means *knowing* more about the Trinity—Father, Son, and Spirit—three in one.

Have you ever watched close friends who finish each other's sentences? Or maybe a couple who've been married for decades moving around the kitchen without words, each anticipating what the other needs? The mystery we call the Trinity has that kind of beautiful love and harmony but infinitely deeper.

People often try to explain the Trinity using everyday objects. "It's like an apple," they say, "with skin, flesh, and core—three distinct parts making one whole." Or, "Think of an egg with its shell, white, and yolk." These simple comparisons help us begin to think about how Father, Son, and Spirit can be distinct yet completely one.

Of course, there's no perfect one-to-one comparison for the beauty and wonder of the Trinity. But one of my favorite ways to think about the Trinity comes from the theological word *perichoresis*. Don't let the fancy term intimidate you. It simply paints an image of the internal relationship of the members of the Trinity like a choreographed dance.

Imagine the most exquisite dance you've ever witnessed, where the dancers move with such unity and joy that you can't always tell where one ends and another begins. That's the Trinity—Father, Son, and Holy Spirit.

Whenever God moves, all the members of the Trinity work together in a delightful dance of mutual admiration, love, and mission, delighting in each other. In this beautiful dance, one member of the Trinity may take the lead, but the others are always in step, completely attuned to each other.

For instance, during creation God the Father took the lead, speaking it into existence, but as Scripture reveals, the Son and Spirit were also actively involved. It was like watching this dance spill over with creativity—all three persons moving together in perfect love to bring something beautiful into being.

Look up the passages and fill in the chart.

Scripture	Role of the Son and of the Spirit
Genesis 1:2	
John 1:1–5, 9–13	
Colossians 1:15–16	

As this divine choreography continues, we see each member of the Trinity stepping forward at different moments while remaining perfectly unified. The music changes, the movement shifts, but the harmony remains unbroken. What began as a dance of creation eventually flows into a dance of restoration.

When I consider the Trinity, I picture a joyous, delightful dance among the Father, Son, and Spirit.

Now, this study will focus on one member of the Trinity, but please note, <u>this is never to be understood as an exclusion of the others</u>. God is one, and where one member of the Trinity is present at work, all of God is present and working. Jesus used a revealing word to describe the Holy Spirit:

> "And I will ask the Father, and he will give you another **advocate**
> to help you and be with you forever."
> John 14:16 (emphasis added)

The original Greek word here is *paraklētos* (sometimes called the "Paraclete"). It literally means "one called to your side," but also connotes a companion who comes to your aid or advocates for you. This paints a picture of someone who comes alongside you, like a trusted friend walking with you on a journey.

Different Bible translations capture various facets of this companionship, calling the Spirit your "Helper," "Counselor," "Comforter," or "Strengthener." Like a diamond with many facets, each name reveals something special about how the Spirit might meet you exactly where you are.

Take a moment to reflect on where you might welcome this divine presence in your life right now. Whether you've known the Spirit for years or are just beginning to explore the Spirit's presence, there's an invitation here for everyone. No pressure—fill in only what resonates with you.

I'm curious about experiencing the Spirit as an **Advocate** (someone who stands up for me) in . . .

I could use a **Helper** (offering practical assistance) with . . .

I'd welcome a **Counselor** (providing wisdom) regarding . . .

I might need a **Comforter** (bringing peace) with . . .

I'd appreciate a **Strengthener** (giving courage) for . . .

This is just a tiny snapshot into the Spirit's presence, like peeking through a keyhole into a vast, beautiful room. There are so many more facets of the Spirit we've yet to explore.

Look up the passages below and fill in the second column with your personal response.

Bible Passage	Work of the Holy Spirt in Our Lives
John 14:25–26	
2 Thessalonians 2:13	
Romans 5:3–5	

Reflecting on the chart above, in which of these areas would you most like the Holy Spirit to do a deeper work in your life? In the space below, write a prayer asking the Spirit to do that work.

This is just an appetizer to the feast of the Holy Spirit's power and presence. The Spirit spans all the centuries of God's story. Just wait until we start digging into the rich flavors of the Old Testament at our next gathering. I can hardly wait for you to taste and see!

PERSONAL STUDY CATCH-UP DAYS 4 & 5

HOLY SPIRIT, TEACH ME MORE

Use these extra days to go back and complete any of the reflection questions or activities from the previous days this week that you were unable to finish. Make note of any insights you've had and make a list of any stories you'd like to share with your group the next time you gather.

> **OPTIONAL:**
>
> Spend the next two days reading chapters 1–2 of the book *The God You Need to Know*. Use the space below and on the next page to note anything in the chapters that stands out to you or encourages your heart.

"When the Spirit steps onto the stage in the opening scene of Genesis, the Spirit doesn't flicker in and out of the chaos of the world. Rather, the *ruach Elohim*—the Spirit of God—hovers over what seems untamable."

FROM *THE GOD YOU NEED TO KNOW*
p. 27

SESSION TWO

THE SPIRIT WHO HOVERS

GROUP STUDY

SCHEDULE

OPTIONAL BEFORE GROUP MEETING	Read chapters 1–2 in *The God You Need to Know* book.
DURING GROUP MEETING	Watch teaching video for Session 2. Group discussion will follow, pages 54–59.
PERSONAL STUDY DAY 1	Study guide pages 61–67
PERSONAL STUDY DAY 2	Study guide pages 68–81
PERSONAL STUDY DAY 3	Study guide pages 82–87
PERSONAL STUDY CATCH-UP DAYS 4 & 5	Complete any unfinished Personal Study activities. Optional: Read chapters 3–4 in *The God You Need to Know* book.

 5–10 minutes

OPENING GROUP DISCUSSION

In the first session, I gave three practices to walk in step with the Spirit and become more attentive to the Holy Spirit, the Paraclete, as Advocate, Helper, Counselor, Comforter, and Strengthener:

- **Marinate in Scripture**
- **Make Space to Listen**
- **Talk About the Holy Spirit with Others**

Go around the group answering a selection of the following questions:

Which practice from our last session did you find most meaningful, and what happened when you tried it?

What surprised you most about incorporating these practices into your daily life?

BONUS

If you haven't already, take a photo of your group and send it to hello@margaretfeinberg.com. Our team would love to see your smiling faces and pray for your group.

 24 minutes

SESSION 2 VIDEO
Leader, stream the video or play the DVD.

> **SCRIPTURE COVERED IN THIS TEACHING SESSION:**
> **Genesis 1:1–2**

VIDEO NOTES
As you watch, use the outline to help you follow along and take notes on anything that stands out to you.

Hidden pictures

Tohu wa vohu means "formless and empty" and speaks of the deep, watery abyss.

Merehephet means "hovering" or "fluttering."

52 The God You Need to Know

Stay alert to the Holy Spirit's hovering.

Engage the Spirit through journaling.

Remain curious with the Spirit.

You can either cling to the crisis or you can cling to Christ, but you do not have arms big enough for both.

If you won't take it away, will you go through it with me?

 30–45 minutes

GROUP DISCUSSION QUESTIONS

Leader note: *Take a few moments to review these questions, then feel free to add some of your own or whisk away any that aren't a good fit for your group. Remember, our goal isn't to cover every question but to foster meaningful discussion and experience those heart-to-heart moments that draw us closer to each other and to God as we journey together—trusting the Spirit to guide our conversations.*

1. What parts of today's teaching either reinforced your perspective, stretched your thinking, or caught your attention?

2. I share, "Rather than withdrawing, the Spirit draws near to the darkness. Rather than retreating, the Spirit advances into the mayhem. Rather than disappearing, the Spirit hovers over the uncertainty and unknown. I have places in my life that are marked by uncertainty and the unknown, that are deep, dark, and chaotic. I think we all do."

The Hebrew phrase tohu wa vohu means "formless and void" and represents the chaos of those places in our lives that are marked by uncertainty or the unknown. What's one chaotic, uncertain, or messy place in your life where you've sensed (or hope to sense) the Spirit's hovering presence?

3. I described how the concept for the cover of this study and book is the idea of "Hidden Pictures" and how the Holy Spirit appears throughout the Old Testament but sometimes is missed or overlooked. Take a moment and look at the cover of the book or the study guide.

   What do you notice tucked into the arrangement besides flowers?

   What's one symbol that represents the Holy Spirit to you that you might tuck into the arrangement on the cover if given the chance?

4. Throughout the Bible, we see the tender loving care of the Father, Son, and Spirit displayed using the imagery of a hovering bird. Select a few volunteers to read Genesis 1:1–2, Deuteronomy 32:10–11, and Luke 13:34.

   What does the eagle and bird imagery of hovering seem to convey about God's attentiveness and love?

Have you ever experienced God's presence like this before? If so, what was it like?

5. **Select a few volunteers to read Psalm 139:7–16.**

   While this is often read thinking about God the Father, how might our understanding change if we consider these words describing the Holy Spirit's presence with us?

6. **God created us with beautiful diversity in how we think, learn, and process the world. Many people describe divine moments of insight, comfort, or guidance in different ways.**

   Thinking back over your life, what's one subtle or surprising moment that you now recognize might have been the Spirit at work?

   What does it tell us about God's character and loving-kindness that the connection with the Spirit might be tailored to each person's unique design rather than requiring everyone to experience God in the same way?

   How can we create a community where different spiritual experiences are honored without making anyone feel they're "doing it wrong" or "less than someone else" if their experience differs from others?

7. Journaling can be a thoughtful way to explore your inner life and spiritual journey no matter where you are in that process.

   Has anyone tried journaling before, whether for personal reflection, creativity, stress relief, or spiritual growth? What was that experience like for you?

   For those who haven't journaled: What aspects of journaling might appeal to you? What hesitations might you have about trying it?

8. As Creator, God can use anything in creation to reach out to us and draw our hearts back to him. I share a story about a white dove visiting a woman's yard on Mother's Day following her husband's death.

   Have you ever had a moment in nature or with something in creation that felt meaningful, comforting, or like a message just for you? If you're comfortable, share what happened and what it meant to you.

   As we conclude this session, what's one specific area in your life where you're excited to invite the Holy Spirit's guidance and presence this week?

BEFORE THE NEXT SESSION...

- Tackle the three days of personal study (and optional two days to catch up and reflect) for Session 2.

- Optional: Read chapters 3–4 of *The God You Need to Know* book.

- Memorize this week's passage using the Scripture memory coloring page. As a bonus, look up the Scripture memory passage in different translations and take note of the variations.

- Try the three practices from this session and be prepared to share how it went at the next gathering.

- For the next session's Opening Group Activity, we're going to celebrate Small Gifts with Bigger Meanings. Ask members to bring something that someone made for them or gave them that was particularly meaningful. If the item is large, have them bring a photo of it on their phone. Consider sending out a reminder to the group about this the night before the next gathering.

CLOSE IN PRAYER

Consider the following prompts as you pray together for:

- Increasing awareness of the Spirit in our *tohu wa vohu*

- A renewed relationship with Holy Spirit—day by day, moment by moment

- Eyes to see and ears to hear the beautiful ways the Spirit is with us

In the beginning God created the heavens and the earth. Now the earth was formless and empty, darkness was over the surface of the deep, and the Spirit of God was hovering over the waters. **Genesis 1:1–2**

SESSION TWO

THE SPIRIT WHO HOVERS

PERSONAL STUDY

PERSONAL STUDY DAY 1

HOLY SPIRIT, HELP ME CATCH MY BREATH

Imagine tracking the most magnificent treasure hunt through the pages of your Bible—from the very first scene where the Spirit hovers over the waters in Genesis 1:2 all the way to the final, wondrous invitation for us to "Come!" in Revelation 22:17. The Holy Spirit is present and active throughout Scripture.

The Old Testament (what Jewish people today call the *Tanakh*) was originally written in ancient Hebrew, and it has a more petite alphabet and vocabulary than other languages. So each word requires broader shoulders to carry more meanings.

Take the word *ruach* (pronounced RU-ach) for instance. Depending on the context, this hardworking word can mean spirit, breath, wind, life force, or even air. That means the same word that describes the gentle brush of a summer breeze also names the Spirit of God.

This is why you might notice something curious when you peek at different Bible translations. The translators had to play detective, looking at the context to decide which meaning of *ruach* fits best in each passage. So in one translation, you might read about God's Spirit moving, while another describes "breath" or "wind" in the exact same verse. It's not a mistake—it's just the beautiful, multifaceted nature of this richly textured word.

Consider Job 27:3-4:

The New International Version reads:

> "As long as I have life within me,
> the **breath of God** in my nostrils,
> my lips will not say anything wicked,
> and my tongue will not utter lies." (emphasis added)

The English Standard Version reads:

> "As long as my breath is in me,
> and the **spirit of God** is in my nostrils,
> my lips will not speak falsehood,
> and my tongue will not utter deceit." (emphasis added)

In this passage, *ruach* can be translated as "breath" or "spirit." That's why sometimes looking for the Holy Spirit in the Old Testament is like looking at one of those "Hidden Pictures" pages in a *Highlights* magazine. We must look closely! And when we do, we're awakened to what the Spirit of God wants to do in us.

In this particular passage, Job is declaring that as long as God gives him life, as long as God gives him breath, as long as the spirit-breath of God is in him, he will utter words of integrity and honesty.

My friend, biblical scholar Jack Levison, notes:

> The Spirit in Job is not the power of victorious living—at least not victorious living in the sense of escape from illness and poverty and grief. The Spirit in Job is not the source of abundant life—at least not abundant life with a permanent smile full of bright white teeth and all the trappings of security and success. . . . The Spirit is simply breath . . . Job is exhausted, winded, we might say: short on God's wind, God's breath, short on God's Spirit. But he has just enough Spirit-breath to open his dry, cracked, dying lips and say [the words of Job 27:3–4].[1]

The heart of this passage isn't about linguistic gymnastics, that is, whether we translate *ruach* as breath, wind, or spirit (though if you're like me and get a little thrill when you discover these delicious Bible details, I see you, fellow word-hunter!). The real question in this passage is . . .

Where are you winded in life? Where are you feeling out of breath?

Job reminds us that the Spirit isn't an emotional espresso shot for spiritual emergencies but rather a way of life, an invitation to experience the Spirit as near as our next breath—whether we're in a season of smooth sailing or caught in the storm of a *tohu wa vohu* (Genesis 1:2).

This traces back to the creation of humankind. Like a skilled potter, God shaped the first human, Adam, from the dust or raw dirt of the ground. Genesis describes:

> Then the LORD God formed a man from the dust of the ground and **breathed** [nishmat chayyim] into his nostrils the **breath of life** [ruach hayyim], and the man became a living being.
> Genesis 2:7 (emphasis added)

The Hebrew word *neshamah* (here spelled *nishmat*) used in this passage also means "breath" and describes the animation of life itself. It captures that moment when dust becomes dancing, thinking, loving humanity. This wasn't just any ordinary puff of air—this was God's own breath, carrying divine DNA into our very being.

It's as if God whispered, "I'll share my very essence with you" and then did exactly that. Every breath you take is a reminder of this first divine exhalation of love.

How would today change if you remembered that you carry this holy breath-gift with every rise and fall of your chest?

When our earthly journey concludes, our dust returns to the earth while our spirit—that divine breath-gift—returns home to the Breath-Giver who shared it in the first place.[2]

> And the dust returns to the ground it came from,
> and the **spirit** returns to God who gave it.
> Ecclesiastes 12:7 (emphasis added)

God's spirit-breath created such a tender, intimate connection with humanity that we can be responsive to the Holy Spirit as close as our next breath.

Jesus embodied this reality when, after the resurrection, he appeared to the disciples and declared "Peace be with you!" (John 20:19). He showed the disciples his wounds and scars and the disciples beamed with joy in his presence.

Look at what happens next:

> Again Jesus said, "Peace be with you! As the Father has sent me,
> I am sending you." And with that he **breathed on them**
> and said, "Receive the Holy Spirit."
> John 20:21–22 (emphasis added)

Notice the parallelism. Just as God breathed into dust to form humanity in Genesis, Jesus now breathes his Spirit directly into his beloved friends.

It's as if Jesus is saying, "This divine connection that I've embodied? It's yours too."

Friend, you weren't accidentally assembled—you were lovingly fashioned, created, and designed for this very relationship with the Holy Spirit. This isn't a distant acquaintance you need special permission to approach. The Spirit isn't playing cosmic hide-and-seek with you or speaking in riddles you can't solve.

The Holy Spirit hovers as close as your next breath, waiting to be noticed, acknowledged, welcomed. If Christ dwells in your heart, then the Spirit already fills your lungs with every breath—the question isn't presence but awareness.

Where in your life right now do you need God's *ruach* to fill your lungs, revive your soul, and infuse you with strength? Take a deep breath right now, and as you exhale, write your heart's honest prayer in the space below.

Remember that on your darkest nights and in your most isolated wilderness the Spirit remains your unwavering companion. This isn't just divine oversight; it's intimate presence. The same power that parted seas and raised Christ dwells within you, turning your ordinary moments into holy ground with every breath you take and step you make.

PERSONAL STUDY DAY 2

HOLY SPIRIT, LET ME EXPERIENCE YOU

Just as the Old Testament word *ruach* possesses many different meanings, the New Testament word for "spirit" also has several different nuances. The ancient Greek word *pneuma* (pronounced NU-ma) not only refers to the Holy Spirit but also to breath, wind, life force, the rational mind or soul, and even angelic beings.

Take for instance Jesus' nighttime conversation with Nicodemus in John 3. Imagine being Nicodemus—respected teacher and religious expert—slipping through the midnight shadows, heart brimming with questions. "How can someone be born when they are old?" he asks Jesus, his logical mind bumping against Jesus' invitation to be born from above (verses 3–4).

Watch how Jesus responds with a smile and some divine wordplay, and underline any phrases that stand out to you:

> "You should not be surprised at my saying, 'You must be born again.' The wind [pneuma] blows wherever it pleases. You hear its sound, but you cannot tell where it comes from or where it is going. So it is with everyone born of the **Spirit** [pneuma]."
> John 3:7–8 (emphasis added)

Notice that Jesus uses *pneuma* twice—once for the unpredictable wind that refuses to follow human schedules or directions, and again for the equally uncontainable Spirit. It's as if Jesus is saying, "Nicodemus, you're trying to map and measure a wild, wonderful mystery that refuses to be contained in your careful categories."

One crucial observation Jesus makes is that like the wind, the Spirit is someone we can experience.

We can't see the wind, but we know it's there.
We can't see the wind, but we can observe its effects.
We can't see the wind, but we can feel its presence.

Now, that does not mean that we run buckshot wild on a whim (Session 4 is all about the loveliness of discernment), but it does mean that as you tend to the Holy Spirit's presence in your life that you're going to have areas where you move from an idea or an abstract thought about God to a living reality. Moments when, as Henry and Richard Blackaby describe, you'll be "experiencing God." [3] And in the process, you'll become even more radiant with Christ.

We must remember that the ways the Spirit works in our lives are unique—just like the colorful patterns of our eyes. If you look in the mirror, you'll see your retina is different than everyone else's on our planet.

We each have different gifts and strengths, personality and interests, so we shouldn't be surprised that Holy Spirit uses different ways to connect with us that are deeply personal and meaningful. Remember what the disciples said after their encounter with Jesus on the road to Emmaus:

> "Were not our **hearts burning within us**
> while he talked with us on the road
> and opened the Scriptures to us?"
> Luke 24:32 (emphasis added)

Just as their encounter with Christ left them with a physical and emotional response, we should not be surprised when we sense or experience the Spirit of the Living God in our hearts, minds, and bodies.

Let's take some time to look at a few of the ways the Holy Spirit interacts with us (there are many more!) and how this is consistent with the work of God throughout Scripture.

HEIGHTENED UNDERSTANDING OF SCRIPTURE

The Holy Spirit brings God's Word alive with meaning and clarity.

What I *la la love* ♥ about this: We don't read or listen to the Scripture alone. The Holy Spirit stands ready to bring God's Word to life in our lives. Through the Holy Spirit, we don't just examine the Bible; the Bible examines us. As 2 Timothy 3:16–17 (MSG) says,

> Every part of Scripture is God-breathed and useful one way or another—showing us truth, exposing our rebellion, correcting our mistakes, training us to live God's way. Through the Word we are put together and shaped up for the tasks God has for us.

Look up the passages listed and fill in the chart.

Scripture	How does the Holy Spirit bring God's Word alive with meaning and clarity?
John 14:26	
1 Thessalonians 1:4–5	

Have you ever had a moment when words from Scripture seemed to speak directly to your situation in a way that felt especially meaningful? What was that experience like for you?

If you're curious about experiencing Scripture in this way, select a passage from this lesson or the previous one and explore it with fresh eyes. Consider taking a moment to read it slowly and prayerfully, with an openness to new insights that might emerge.

INNER PEACE

The Holy Spirit brings a deep sense of peace.

What I *la la love* ♥ about this: The peace that God gives is unlike anything the world can offer—it is a deep, unshakable peace that surpasses all understanding. This divine peace comes through God's presence and promises alongside the Spirit working in our hearts. And this peace has a purpose!

As you read the following passages, underline or circle anything that reveals the Holy Spirit bringing peace.

> May the God of hope fill you
> with all joy and **peace** as you trust in him,
> so that you may overflow with hope
> by the power of the **Holy Spirit**.
> Romans 15:13 (emphasis added)

So the church throughout all Judea and Galilee and Samaria
had **peace** and was being built up. And walking in the fear of the Lord
and in the comfort of the **Holy Spirit**, it multiplied.
Acts 9:31 (ESV, emphasis added)

Be completely humble and gentle; be patient, bearing with one
another in love. Make every effort to keep the unity of the **Spirit**
through the bond of **peace**.
Ephesians 4:2–3 (emphasis added)

Reflecting on these passages, what connections do you see between the Holy Spirit's presence and peace?

Have you ever experienced the Holy Spirit filling you with a deep sense of peace? If so, describe.

If you're curious about exploring this kind of deep peace in your life, what situation currently feels most in need? Consider taking a quiet, prayerful moment to reflect on what peace might look like in that context and ask the Holy Spirit to give you deep peace.

BOLDNESS AND STRENGTH

The Holy Spirit empowers people to act courageously.

What I *la la love* ♥ about this: Often I'm a scaredy cat when it comes to sharing my faith. I fear saying the wrong thing, so I'm tempted to say nothing at all. But the Helper stands by to empower us, to fill us with courage and boldness, so we can share the fabulous news of Jesus and his kingdom with compassion and kindness.

Look up the passages listed and fill in the chart.

Scripture	How did the Holy Spirit impart physical and spiritual boldness and strength in each of these passages?
Judges 14:6	
Acts 4:31	

Think about a time when you needed to be brave or strong. Where did you find the courage to move forward? Was there a moment when you felt empowered by the Spirit beyond what you thought possible? If so, describe.

If you're interested in developing more courage in your life, what situation currently challenges you? What might it look like to approach that situation with a sense of being led and carried by the Holy Spirit and knowing you're not alone?

EMOTIONAL AND PHYSICAL RESPONSES

The Holy Spirit stirs our hearts and bodies toward a righteous response to God.

What I *la la love* ♥ about this: For me, it's easy to love God with my mind, to think about and ponder the wonders of God. But we're also meant to love God with our whole body, soul, and strength. So we should not be surprised when the Living God infuses our mind, body, soul, and strength with the echoing reality that the Spirit is in us, with us, and reminding us that God will never leave us nor forsake us (Deuteronomy 31:8).

Look up the passages listed and fill in the chart.

Scripture	How did the Holy Spirit stir hearts or physical response toward God?
Ezekiel 3:14–15	
Isaiah 61:1–3	
Luke 10:21	

Have you ever had a powerful moment that affected you emotionally or physically—perhaps a sense of peace, joy, or even goose bumps while talking about God? What was that like for you?

Many people find that meaningful spiritual experiences engage not just the intellect but also emotions and even physical sensations. Across Scripture there are accounts of profound spiritual encounters that involve someone's whole being—mind, emotions, and body—working together. Transformative experiences like these often involve more than just thinking—they can touch every aspect of who we are.

If you're curious about loving and experiencing God more, what might help you engage with the Lord beyond just intellectually?

DREAMS AND VISUAL IMAGES

The Holy Spirit communicates through dreams and their interpretations as well as visions.

What I *la la love* ♥ about this: I write about this in depth in chapter 3 of *The God You Need to Know* book when I explore the life of Joseph. The Spirit sometimes uses sleep to say to us things we cannot receive as readily while we are awake. One of the loveliest aspects of the Holy Spirit speaking to us through dreams (or visual images) is that it's all a gift. We can't make ourselves dream or force an encounter with God. We can't work harder to earn any of it. These tender encounters with the Spirit of the Living God don't happen every night, and they don't happen in every season. I can't even explain exactly how they happen. All I know is that they do sometimes.

Look up the passages listed and fill in the chart.

Scripture	How did the Holy Spirit use dreams, and their interpretation, or visions in these passages?
Genesis 37:5–9; 41:14–33	
Ezekiel 8:3	
Acts 2:17 (quoting Joel 2:28)	

Describe a moment of unexpected clarity or insight that felt divinely inspired. How did you recognize it as potentially from God?

If you're interested in paying more attention to your dreams or moments of divine insight, what practices might help you become more receptive to them?

CONVICTION OF SIN

The Holy Spirit relieves us of our wrongdoing with God.

What I *la la love* ♥ about this: The Holy Spirit reveals where we've gone amiss not as condemnation or as a source of shame but rather as an invitation to live into the fullness of the life God intends. The Spirit spurs us toward goodness and righteousness so we can look more like Jesus and mature into all God has for us.

As you read the following passages, underline or circle anything that reveals the Holy Spirit unveiling sin and spurring people toward righteousness.

> "I will give you a new heart and put a new spirit in you;
> I will remove from you your heart of stone and give you a heart of flesh.
> And I will put my **Spirit** in you and move you to follow my decrees
> and be careful to keep my laws."
> Ezekiel 36:26–27 (emphasis added)

> When the people heard this, they were cut to the heart
> and said to Peter and the other apostles, "Brothers, what shall we do?"
> Peter replied, "Repent and be baptized, every one of you,
> in the name of Jesus Christ for the forgiveness of your sins.
> And you will receive the gift of the **Holy Spirit**."
> Acts 2:37–38 (emphasis added)

Draw a symbol below that represents a time when you sensed conviction in your life and the Holy Spirit spurring you toward righteousness.

How did the Spirit's gentle nudge toward repentance lead you toward positive change? How did that transformation unfold?

If you haven't yet experienced the Spirit spurring you toward righteousness, simply ask for this gift now.

WISDOM AND GUIDANCE IN DECISIONS

The Holy Spirit provides wisdom and guidance to navigate life.

What I *la la love* ♥ about this: Life presents us with countless decisions ranging from major life choices to everyday crossroads. All the macro- and micro-decisions of life can feel overwhelming at times. The good news is that we do not face them alone. We have our Advocate and Counselor whom we can call on for wisdom, direction, and guidance. And we can move forward knowing that even if we misstep, Holy Spirit is faithful and true to lead us back to the best path.

Look up the passages listed and fill in the chart.

Scripture	How does the Holy Spirit provide wisdom and guidance?
Isaiah 11:2	
Acts 13:2–4	
1 Corinthians 2:10–12	

Think of a decision where you sensed divine guidance. What made you confident it was the Spirit's direction rather than just your own preferences?

If you've never experienced the Holy Spirit providing wisdom and guidance as you navigate through life, ask the Spirit to work in your life in this way.

Each of us is uniquely made, with different ways of experiencing the world around us. It makes sense that our spiritual experiences would be just as diverse. The invitation is simply to remain attentive to the Spirit's presence and work in our lives.

PERSONAL STUDY DAY 3

HOLY SPIRIT, I WANT TO BE MORE ATTENTIVE TO YOU

One of the practices that can make us more attentive to the Spirit is simply writing things down. As I shared in this session's video teaching, I've been slow to take up journaling. After I write all day, the last thing I want to do is write some more.

I'm grateful for friends who have challenged me to grow in this area and use a journal as a place to be more mindful of the Holy Spirit throughout my day. When we engage the Spirit through journaling, it can become a place where we can start conversations with the Holy Spirit and remain curious with the Spirit all at the same time.

Now, some of you may be thinking, *Why do I need to start a conversation with Holy Spirit? Won't the Spirit just speak to me?*

Yes, the Spirit is a living gift of grace who will speak and lead and guide you. But Holy Spirit doesn't want a *transaction* with you. Holy Spirit wants a *delightful, joyous relationship* with you.

And what makes a good relationship? Asking questions. Staying curious. Listening attentively. Being grateful. Engaging in conversation. Enjoying each other.

Imagine starting your day with a question that follows you like a gentle companion—not demanding but just quietly present as you move through your hours.

This is what happened when I began a practice so simple I almost dismissed it—asking the Holy Spirit one question each morning. It looks like this:

Each morning, I open my journal and write a single question/statement at the top of the page—an invitation to conversation:

- *What do I most need to hear from you today?*
- *Will you make me more like Jesus?*
- *Help me recognize your presence today.*
- *Who are you calling me to love?*
- *What's on your heart?*

Then I wait, pen hovering over paper. Sometimes what comes is just a fragment—a passage of Scripture that bubbles up, the chorus of a song I haven't thought about in months, or simply an impression that feels different from my usual mental chatter. I write it down without editing or second-guessing myself.

This question becomes my day's companion. While driving, I remember it. Standing in line for coffee, it returns. During a challenging conversation, it whispers in the background.

Often, what happens the next morning surprises me. Before asking a new question, I return to yesterday's page and add notes—moments of unexpected clarity, a conversation that seemed oddly relevant to my question, or sometimes just "nothing remarkable noticed." Both the profound and the ordinary get recorded.

What's happened over time has astonished me. Flipping through pages of these simple exchanges, I've discovered a conversation I didn't know I was having—patterns of guidance so subtle I would have missed them if not captured on paper.

The Spirit's voice wasn't thundering from mountaintops but whispering and echoing through ordinary Tuesdays.

> My heart is stirred by a noble theme
> as I recite my verses for the king;
> my tongue is the pen of a skillful writer.
> Psalm 45:1

I dare you to try this for the next few days. Grab whatever's handy—a proper journal, the back of an envelope, the notes app on your phone, or the space we've provided in the following pages. Choose one question that resonates with you or create your own. Write down whatever comes to mind, without judgment. Then carry that question through your day like a treasure hunt.

You might experience profound insight . . . or nothing at all. Some days my page stays nearly blank! But persist anyway. The beauty isn't in dramatic daily revelations but in the gentle unfolding of a relationship over time.

What begins as an experiment often becomes a lifeline—a simple practice that trains our attention to notice the Holy Spirit already moving through our everyday moments.

What question is stirring in your heart right now? The page is open, the pen is ready, and the conversation is waiting to begin.

DATE:

PRAYER PROMPT:
_____
_____
_____
_____
_____
_____
_____
_____
_____
_____
_____

DATE:

PRAYER PROMPT:
_____
_____
_____
_____
_____
_____
_____
_____
_____
_____
_____

DATE:

PRAYER PROMPT:

_____
_____
_____
_____
_____
_____
_____
_____
_____
_____

DATE:

PRAYER PROMPT:

_____
_____
_____
_____
_____
_____
_____
_____
_____
_____

DATE:

PRAYER PROMPT:

DATE:

PRAYER PROMPT:

PERSONAL STUDY CATCH-UP DAYS 4 & 5

HOLY SPIRIT, TEACH ME MORE

Use these extra days to go back and complete any of the reflection questions or activities from the previous days this week that you couldn't finish. Make note of any insights you've had and make a list of any stories you'd like to share with your group the next time you gather.

> **OPTIONAL:**
>
> Spend the next two days reading chapters 3–4 of the book *The God You Need to Know*. Use the space below and on the next page to note anything in the chapters that stands out to you or encourages your heart.

"Long before Aaron entered the holy of holies, the Spirit of the Living God had been refining the skills of the artists and artisans. . . . The Spirit had 'filled' Bezalel and Oholiab with brilliance and insight 'to make' and teach others 'to make. . .' The Spirit had been bringing together people with diverse gifts and talents to accomplish something extraordinary and sacred. And the Spirit continues to delight in doing so today."

FROM *THE GOD YOU NEED TO KNOW*
p.64

SESSION THREE

THE SPIRIT WHO MAKES

GROUP STUDY

SCHEDULE

OPTIONAL BEFORE GROUP MEETING	Read chapters 3–4 in *The God You Need to Know* book.
DURING GROUP MEETING	Watch teaching video for Session 3. Group discussion will follow, pages 96–101.
PERSONAL STUDY DAY 1	Study guide pages 103–110
PERSONAL STUDY DAY 2	Study guide pages 111–116
PERSONAL STUDY DAY 3	Study guide pages 117–124
PERSONAL STUDY CATCH-UP DAYS 4 & 5	Complete any unfinished Personal Study activities. Optional: Read chapters 5–6 in *The God You Need to Know* book.

 5–10 minutes

OPENING GROUP DISCUSSION

SMALL GIFTS WITH BIGGER MEANINGS

Invite participants to hold up the item or gift of particular meaning they brought and then share the following:

Say what the item is and who gave it to you.

In one sentence, describe what made this gift meaningful.

In the last session, I gave three practices to walk in step with the Spirit in our *tohu wa vohu*—those places of uncertainty, the unknown, the chaos that sometimes erupts in our lives:

- **Stay Alert to Holy Spirit's Hovering**
- **Engage the Spirit Through Journaling**
- **Remain Curious with the Spirit**

Discuss the following:

How did experimenting with last week's practices impact your awareness of the Spirit? Share a specific moment if possible.

BONUS

Take a photo of some of the items and send them to hello@margaretfeinberg.com. Our team would love to see what you brought.

 25 minutes

SESSION 3 VIDEO

Leader, stream the video or play the DVD.

> **SCRIPTURE COVERED IN THIS TEACHING SESSION:**
> Exodus 31:1–7; 35:34; 38:23

VIDEO NOTES

As you watch, use the outline to help you follow along and take notes on anything that stands out to you.

Sometimes when you have a God-given passion, it's not something you run toward as much as it's something you can't run away from.

The holy hum of God's presence

The tabernacle

Bezalel and Oholiab

You are a maker . . . it may just look different.

Breathe prayer as naturally as air.

The Jesus Prayer: Breathe in: *Lord Jesus Christ, Son of God.* Breathe out: *Have mercy on me.*

Surrender perfection.

Susie's pieces

 30–45 minutes

GROUP DISCUSSION QUESTIONS

Leader note: *Take a few moments to review these questions, then feel free to add some of your own or whisk away any that aren't a good fit for your group. Remember, our goal isn't to cover every question but to foster meaningful discussion and experience those heart-to-heart moments that draw us closer to each other and to God as we journey together—trusting the Spirit to guide our conversations.*

1. What's lingering in your mind after today's teaching—perhaps something that inspired you, challenged a previously held view, or just caught your attention?

2. I sometimes experience what I call the "holy hum of God's presence" when I write. In the 1981 film *Chariots of Fire,* the actor who portrays Olympic runner Eric Liddell famously says, "When I run, I feel God's pleasure."

    Ask everyone to close their eyes for a moment and imagine doing something that brings them deep satisfaction or joy. After thirty seconds, invite them to open their eyes and turn to a neighbor (or everyone, depending on your group size) to share briefly what they imagined.

How might these moments of deep satisfaction connect with the concept of the holy hum of God's pleasure or the Holy Spirit's presence?

3. Has there been a time when you were ready to give up on something important, but somehow the Holy Spirit gave you the courage or inspiration to continue? If so, describe.

4. Before reading the passage, ask participants to count off by threes. Give each group a different assignment:

    Group 1: Listen for all the different <u>items</u> mentioned.

    Group 2: Listen for all the different <u>skills</u> mentioned or implied.

    Now, ask volunteers to take turns reading Exodus 31:1–7 and 38:23. Then discuss:

    Let's hear from each group what they noticed. (Invite groups to report.)

    What surprises you about the variety of talents needed for building the tabernacle?

Why do you think the biblical text goes into such detail about these skills and crafts? What might that suggest about how these activities were valued?

5. I share, "Now you may be thinking, *I'm not a maker, I don't make anything.* I want to challenge you: You are a maker; it just may look different. Think of those who helped develop systems, provide logistics, and transport raw material. Those who helped gather the offering, count it, weigh it, measure it . . . Those who watched the children, prepared the meals, helped with cleanup. All those people were involved in the process of making . . . it possible."

How have your strengths, talents, or ways of thinking contributed to something larger than yourself? (This could be at work, in your family, in a community project, etc.)

Think of something you've helped "make possible" for others.
What did that experience teach you about your unique contributions?

Looking around your group, what different kinds of "makers" do you see represented here? How might our diverse abilities complement each other?

6. What has been your experience with breath prayer before today, if any? (For those new to this practice, what was your initial reaction just now?)

For those who tried saying breath prayers during the video, what surprised you about the experience? Did anything feel particularly meaningful or challenging?

What might make you curious to explore breath prayer further? Or what questions do you have about this practice?

7. Let's explore a scripture that offers a different perspective on our work and creativity. Ask someone to read Psalm 90:17 aloud. If your group feels comfortable, invite the group to try it as a breath prayer together.

Breathe in: May the favor of the Lord our God rest on us
Breathe out: Establish the work of our hands for us
Breathe in: Yes, establish
Breathe out: The work of our hands

How might this passage offer an alternative to perfectionism?

What shifts when we see our work as something God "establishes" rather than something we must perfect?

How might this passage help us move from duty to delight as makers?

8. The story I shared about Susie's flower pieces reminds us how objects can carry deep meaning beyond their physical form. Looking back at the opening activity, are any of these items marked by a *permanence* or *meaning* that goes beyond the object itself? If so, which ones?

How might welcoming the Holy Spirit into our creative processes—whether making art, preparing presentations, organizing spaces, or solving problems—change our relationship with the work itself? And with the Spirit?

BEFORE THE NEXT SESSION...

- Tackle the three days of personal study (and optional two days to catch up and reflect) for Session 3.

- Optional: Read chapters 5–6 of *The God You Need to Know* book.

- Memorize this week's passage using the Scripture memory coloring page. As a bonus, look up the Scripture memory passage in different translations and take note of the variations.

- Try the three practices from this session and be prepared to share how it went at the next gathering.

CLOSE IN PRAYER

Consider the following prompts as you pray together for:

- Moments to breathe prayer as naturally as air
- The Lord to establish the work of your hands
- Opportunities to delight in the Spirit

Then the LORD said to Moses, "See, I have chosen Bezalel son of Uri, the son of Hur, of the tribe of Judah, and I have filled him with the Spirit of God, with wisdom, with understanding, with knowledge and with all kinds of skills—to make artistic designs." **Exodus 31:1–4**

SESSION THREE

THE SPIRIT WHO MAKES

PERSONAL STUDY

PERSONAL STUDY DAY 1

HOLY SPIRIT, GIVE ME YOUR WISDOM, UNDERSTANDING, AND KNOWLEDGE

Picture this: a portable sanctuary shimmering with gold, vibrant with color, and fragrant with incense traveling across desert sands alongside the Israelites. This was more than a religious construction project. This divine pop-up tent allowed the presence of God to travel right in their midst. And who did God tap to create this masterpiece? Two artisans with wonderfully meaningful names:

Bezalel means "in the shadow of God," and the name **Oholiab** means "father's tent."

These weren't just craftsmen—they were Spirit-filled creators who made the world more beautiful through the work of their hands.

What specific things does God fill Bezalel with? Circle all that apply and add any I missed.

- Holy Spirit
- Wisdom
- Technical skill
- Divine inspiration
- Understanding
- Knowledge
- Creativity
- _____

Notice how the Bible often groups **wisdom, understanding, and knowledge** together like best friends who never leave each other's side. These aren't just random qualities—they're gifts God delights in giving.

Read Proverbs 3:19–20. How did this powerful trio of wisdom, understanding, and knowledge show up during the original creation of . . . well, everything?

Now, these gifts don't just come from God as random talents—they're rooted in relationship with God:

> The fear of the LORD is the beginning of wisdom,
> and knowledge of the Holy One is understanding.
> Proverbs 9:10

The apostle Paul was so excited about these gifts that he couldn't stop praying for believers to be filled with them through the Holy Spirit.

Read Colossians 1:9–12 below and grab a colorful pen or pencil. Underline, circle, or highlight everything that happens when we're filled with knowledge, wisdom, and understanding by the Spirit.

> For this reason, since the day we heard about you, we have not stopped praying for you. We continually ask God to fill you with the knowledge of his will through all the wisdom and understanding that the Spirit gives, so that you may live a life worthy of the Lord and please him in every way: bearing fruit in every good work, growing in the knowledge of God, being strengthened with all power according to his glorious might so that you may have great endurance and patience, and giving joyful thanks to the Father, who has qualified you to share in the inheritance of his holy people in the kingdom of light.
>
> Colossians 1:9–12

How would inviting the Spirit to give you knowledge, wisdom, and understanding in your work transform the outcome?

What project or task are you currently working on that you've been trying to muscle through on your own? (We all have them!)

How might the Spirit's wisdom transform this situation?

Right now—yes, this very moment—take a breath and ask the Holy Spirit for wisdom, understanding, and knowledge for something you'll be working on soon. It could be a work project, a difficult conversation, a creative endeavor, or even something as ordinary as organizing your kitchen.

After you pray:

- Notice your posture toward the Spirit. Any shifts in your approach?
- Pay attention to what might bubble up.
- If you're keeping that prayer journal we talked about earlier, jot down any new thoughts or insights that might surface.

Along with being filled with the Spirit of God, wisdom, knowledge, understanding, and skills, Bezalel and Oholiab were also given "the ability to teach others" (Exodus 35:34).

The gifts of wisdom, knowledge, understanding, and skills weren't just given *to* them; they were meant to *flow through* them. Their creativity came with contagious generosity attached.

If you've ever tried to lead creatives, you know it's easier to herd cats through a waterfall. Yet the Spirit—whom Jesus later nicknames "the Helper"—empowers Bezalel and Oholiab to lead an entire guild of artisans. Rather than hoard their skills or bask in the pride of their creative talents, Bezalel and Oholiab welcome others to participate in the work and further develop their own giftings.

This week, notice one way you could let the Spirit's gifts flow through you to someone else. Is there a skill you could teach? Wisdom you could share? Understanding you could offer?

Write down one small step you'll take to be a "flow-through" creator.

This beautiful "flow-through" principle didn't stop with tabernacle artisans. Fast-forward to the early church and we see the same Spirit creating something equally stunning—a community where generosity and unity flourished like wildflowers after rain.

Read Acts 2:42–47. How did the Holy Spirit spark generosity and unity among members of the early church? Note the specific actions or attitudes you discover in the space below.

Describe a time when you've sensed the Spirit drawing you toward generosity or unity.

How did that experience impact your faith?

No matter what you're making—whether it's a spreadsheet or a sonnet, a casserole or a corporate strategy—your work is laced with opportunities to awaken to the Spirit's presence.

Every task, no matter how ordinary, can become extraordinary when infused with the Spirit's wisdom, understanding, knowledge, and skill. And every interaction holds potential for a radical kind of generosity and unity wherever you go.

So as you journey through your week, may you remember to pause and pray, "Holy Spirit, give me your wisdom, knowledge, and understanding."

May your hands become extensions of the Maker's hands, your mind illuminated by the Spirit's insight, and your heart quickened by opportunities to experience the joy of Spirit-led generosity. The same Spirit who empowered Bezalel and Oholiab awaits you today.

PERSONAL STUDY DAY 2

HOLY SPIRIT, SATURATE ME IN YOUR LOVE

Today, we're peeking into an oft-overlooked passage where the Holy Spirit shows up in the Old Testament, and how it challenges us to look for the Spirit in delightfully unexpected people and places. The story begins with our friend Moses at his wit's end with the constant complaints of the Israelites during their wilderness wandering.

Read Numbers 11:10–17. What specific concerns does Moses bring to God? (This is quite the honest prayer.)

How does God respond to Moses's burnout crisis? What's the solution?

Remember our friends Bezalel and Oholiab? The tabernacle project was too immense for Bezalel alone, so the Spirit stirred up a whole guild of artisans to help. Now we see the same pattern: Moses' leadership load has become crushingly heavy, and once again the Spirit steps in to spread the weight across more shoulders.

We often think of the Paraclete, the Holy Spirit, as our Helper, which is wonderfully true, but there's something even bigger happening. The Spirit works through *community*, bringing people together to accomplish God's purposes and build God's kingdom.

Where in your life do you most need the Holy Spirit to bring others alongside you to share a burden that feels too heavy to carry alone?

Listen quietly for a moment. Where might the Spirit be nudging you to come alongside someone else who's carrying too much alone?

Read Numbers 11:24–25. What happens when the Spirit rests on the elders?

Now here's where the story takes a surprising turn. According to Numbers 11:26-27, among the elders are two outliers—Eldad and Medad—who don't follow Moses' instruction to gather at the tent. The Bible doesn't explain why:

- Perhaps they were handling an emergency in camp?
- Maybe they'd grown frustrated with Moses or the food situation?
- Or what if they were distracted with a sand-building competition?

We don't know why. But here's the marvelous part—the Holy Spirit includes them anyway.

> However, two men, whose names were Eldad and Medad, had remained in the camp. They were listed among the elders, but did not go out to the tent. Yet the Spirit also rested on them, and they prophesied in the camp. A young man ran and told Moses, "Eldad and Medad are prophesying in the camp."
>
> Numbers 11:26–27

Why does this story matter so much? Because we're exploring practices to deepen our relationship with the Holy Spirit. Each is designed to help you become more attentive so you can delight in the Spirit and enjoy the Spirit's presence. But we must remember that the Spirit is fundamentally a gift of grace. We cannot work or earn the Spirit's favor or presence.

Like with Eldad and Medad, even when we're distracted or miss the message, the Spirit remains faithful and can pour out power regardless of what we do or leave undone.

Eldad's and Medad's names come from the Hebrew root *ydd*, meaning "to love."

- **Eldad** can be translated "God has loved."
- **Medad** can be translated "object of affection."

The power of the Spirit is poured out on those God has loved and those who are the objects of divine affection. That's us!

What comfort do you find in knowing the power of the Spirit isn't based on what you do or leave undone but rather on God's wild, relentless love for you?

Read Ephesians 3:16–19. What is the source of the power to comprehend the boundless love of God?

How have you sensed the Holy Spirit revealing God's love to you recently? (This could be through people, circumstances, creation, Scripture, an inner awareness, etc.)

Now, not everyone recognizes the beauty of the Spirit's unexpected work.

Read Numbers 11:28–29. How does Joshua respond when he hears about Eldad and Medad prophesying? And how does Moses respond to Joshua's concerns?

Moses' response to Joshua is gloriously generous and selfless. He recognizes that the Spirit's power isn't just for a select few but is for everyone. This longing echoes throughout Scripture from Joel's prophecy (Joel 2:28-29) to Paul's wish that all might prophesy (1 Corinthians 14:5).

As you go through your week, keep your eyes open for the "Eldads and Medads" in your life—places and people where the Spirit might be working in unexpected, unconventional ways. The Holy Spirit loves to color outside our carefully drawn lines.

Where is the Spirit challenging your assumptions about how God works?

Remember this: The Spirit who rested on the elders in Numbers 11, both those who followed instructions and those who didn't, is the same Spirit who rests on you today—not because you've earned it, but because you are deeply, wildly loved.

PERSONAL STUDY DAY 3

HOLY SPIRIT, WORK IN MY LIFE *TO THE NTH DEGREE*

Sometimes it's tempting to think of the Spirit appearing in dramatic fashion, like prophets caught up in divine visions. But what about living with the Spirit day after day, year after year, through changing circumstances and shifting political landscapes?

Enter Daniel—a man whose Spirit-filled life spanned decades and dynasties. His story challenges us to see that walking with the Spirit isn't about mountaintop moments as much as the long, faithful journey through valleys and plains.

When King Nebuchadnezzar of Babylon conquered Jerusalem, he took select young Israelites to serve in his court. Among them were four friends from noble families: Daniel, Hananiah, Mishael, and Azariah. Renamed Belteshazzar, Shadrach, Meshach, and Abednego, they entered Babylon's three-year royal training program.

Read Daniel 1:4. Why were these men selected?

While it would have likely been easier to just cave in and follow the crowd, Daniel and his friends resolved not to defile themselves with the king's food and wine. Rather than rebelling outright, he diplomatically requested a test:

> "Please test your servants for ten days:
> Give us nothing but vegetables to eat and water to drink.
> Then compare our appearance with that of the young men
> who eat the royal food, and treat your servants
> in accordance with what you see."
>
> Daniel 1:12–13

After ten days, the four friends looked healthier than those eating the royal diet. The official allowed them to continue their chosen diet. The scripture notes that God gave Daniel & Co. some of the same gifts Bezalel and Oholiab received.

> God gave these four young men **knowledge** and
> **understanding** in every kind of literature and wisdom.
> Daniel also understood **visions** and **dreams** of every kind.
>
> Daniel 1:17 (CSB, emphasis added)

Reflecting on Daniel 1:17, what did God give Daniel and his friends according to this passage?

Which of these gifts did Bezalel also enjoy according to Exodus 31:3?

Now, these spiritual gifts aren't necessarily brand spanking new. Remember, these men are selected from the first because they're "suitable for instruction in *all wisdom, knowledgeable, perceptive, and capable*" (Daniel 1:4 CSB, emphasis added). The Spirit enhances the gifts he's already placed within them. This supernatural wisdom and understanding even empowers Daniel to interpret every vision and dream.

God doesn't remove the foursome from their circumstances; He meets them in their circumstances. He gives them *exceedingly more* of what they'll need, not just for that moment but for what is to come.

This spiritual enrichment becomes impossible to miss.

Read Daniel 1:20. When the king examines the young nobles three years later, what does he find in Daniel and his friends?

King Nebuchadnezzar appoints the foursome to his court. Daniel is chosen governor of Babylon, and Shadrach, Meshach, and Abednego serve alongside him. Sometime later, the king has a nightmare, and Daniel interprets the dream. Throughout this process, the king recognizes the Spirit of God working within Daniel:

> "The **spirit of the holy gods** is in him."
> Daniel 4:8 (emphasis added)

> "I know that the **spirit of the holy gods** is in you."
> Daniel 4:9 (emphasis added)

> "The **spirit of the holy gods** is in you."
> Daniel 4:18 (emphasis added)

This profound observation isn't just a one and done; it continues echoing among future Babylonian kings as well.

When Belshazzar throws a celebratory feast using the chalices stolen from the temple in Jerusalem, a mysterious hand writes something cryptic and nightmarish that leaves the king wobbly and knock-kneed.

Read Daniel 5:9–12. Even amid terror at Belshazzar's feast, who remembers Daniel and why?

What specific qualities does the queen attribute to Daniel, and what is their source according to her?

Belshazzar summons Daniel and offers him lavish rewards for interpreting the mysterious handwriting. Despite delivering devastating news, Daniel's wisdom is recognized.

That very night, the kingdom of Babylon falls to Darius the Mede, and Belshazzar is killed. Yet Daniel's Spirit-filled reputation continues to precede him.

Read Daniel 6:1–3. How does the new king, Darius, view Daniel? What is specifically mentioned as the reason for Daniel's distinction?

Throughout the book of Daniel, we encounter a small Aramaic adjective that's easy to overlook but carries enormous significance: *yattir*. While often translated simply as "excellent," this word conveys something far more powerful—it speaks of what's being described to the utmost.

Let's explore how this word appears throughout Daniel:

- Nebuchadnezzar's golden statue has brightness described as *yattir*—so exceedingly intense that it's blinding (2:31).
- The furnace heated for Shadrach, Meshach, and Abednego is *yattir*—so hot it kills those who approach it (3:22).
- When Nebuchadnezzar returns to the throne, his majesty is *yattir*—exceedingly greater than before (4:36).
- Daniel's terrifying vision of the fourth beast is *yattir*—exceedingly dreadful (7:7, 19).

My friend, biblical scholar Jack Levison, suggests that translating *yattir* as "excellent" is just too tame. The word is exponential in its expression of quality, quantity, intensity, and capacity. *Yattir* is better translated as "to the nth degree."[4]

- The blinding brightness of golden statue is to the nth degree.
- The heat of the furnace is to the nth degree.
- The majesty of the king is restored to the nth degree.
- The dread of the fourth beast is to the nth degree.

Of the eight times this word appears in Daniel, three of them describe Daniel himself:

- Daniel has a ruach yattirah, "an exceptional spirit" (5:12).
- Daniel has hokmah yattirah, "exceptional wisdom," in him (5:14).
- Daniel receives a high position because he had a ruach yattira, "an exceptional spirit" (6:4).

What might it look like for you to experience the Spirit "to the nth degree" in your life?

Unlike many Spirit-filled figures in Scripture, we don't read about a dramatic moment when the Spirit came upon Daniel. Instead, we see a consistent Spirit presence throughout his life—from his youth into his old age, spanning multiple kingdoms and rulers. Daniel's experience helps us see the work of God's Spirit over the long haul.

Read Daniel 6:10 and 10:2–3. What specific spiritual practices do we see in Daniel's life?

How might these practices have contributed to Daniel's and others' awareness of the presence of the Spirit "to the nth degree" in his life?

Daniel could have easily given in to the power games, politics, and competition that circled the king's court. Instead, he resisted the machinery of the empire and focused on faithfulness to God.

In what specific area is the Spirit prompting you to resist worldly conformity?

Daniel's story challenges our tendency to want something new from the Spirit—new experiences, new places, new feelings. While God does make all things new, sometimes we long for the Spirit to do something fresh when he's already been working faithfully where we are for a very long time.

As we reflect on Daniel's Spirit-filled life, consider the following:

What aspect of Daniel's relationship with the Spirit most challenges your own spiritual journey?

Daniel maintained his spiritual integrity across decades and through dramatic cultural shifts. What would it look like for you to remain faithful to the Spirit's leading through the next major transition in your life?

Let's close in prayer:

Spirit of the Living God, we invite you to work in our lives "to the nth degree." Like Daniel, may we set our hearts to gain understanding and to humble ourselves before you. Help us to resist the temptations of worldly power and success, choosing instead the path of faithful obedience day after day. May our lives—through changing seasons and circumstances—consistently reflect your presence, wisdom, and power. Amen.

PERSONAL STUDY CATCH-UP DAYS 4 & 5

HOLY SPIRIT, TEACH ME MORE

Use these extra days to go back and complete any of the reflection questions or activities from the previous days this week that you were unable to finish. Make note of any insights you've had and make a list of any stories you'd like to share with your group the next time you gather.

> **OPTIONAL:**
>
> Spend the next two days reading chapters 5–6 of the book *The God You Need to Know*. Use the space below to note anything in the chapters that stands out to you or encourages your heart.

"We must start by using Scripture to scrutinize any words we suspect are prompted by the Spirit. If the syllables are Spirit-given, then they'll never conflict with Scripture or the character of God. And even when the words are aligned with both, the discernment process has just begun. We must also check our hearts to ensure that our speech and the tone we use reflect the compassion and love of God."

FROM *THE GOD YOU NEED TO KNOW*
p. 103

SESSION FOUR

THE BEAUTY OF DISCERNMENT

GROUP STUDY

SCHEDULE

OPTIONAL BEFORE GROUP MEETING	Read chapters 5–6 in *The God You Need to Know* book.
DURING GROUP MEETING	Watch teaching video for Session 4. Group discussion will follow, pages 132–137.
PERSONAL STUDY DAY 1	Study guide pages 139–147
PERSONAL STUDY DAY 2	Study guide pages 148–158
PERSONAL STUDY DAY 3	Study guide pages 159–167
PERSONAL STUDY CATCH-UP DAYS 4 & 5	Complete any unfinished Personal Study activities. Optional: Read chapters 7–8 in *The God You Need to Know* book.

 5–10 minutes

OPENING GROUP DISCUSSION

In the third session, I gave two practices to walk in step with the Spirit in whatever you set your head, hand, or heart to make:

- **Breathe Prayer as Naturally as Air**
- **Surrender Perfectionism**

Go around the group answering a selection of the following questions:

As you've tried these spiritual practices, have you noticed any patterns in how the Spirit seems to communicate most clearly with you?

What unexpected benefits or challenges have emerged from these practices?

Did anything surprising, delightful, or difficult happen when you tried one of these? If so, describe.

 26 minutes

SESSION 4 VIDEO
Leader, stream the video or play the DVD.

> **SCRIPTURE COVERED IN THIS TEACHING SESSION:**
> Judges 6:12–24, 33–34; 1 Samuel 6:12; 2 Samuel 23:1–2; Matthew 23:34

VIDEO NOTES
As you watch, use the outline to help you follow along and take notes on anything that stands out to you.

Gideon

Humility, unassuming nature

Far less concerned with the *me* as he was with the *we*

Brings his toughest questions and deepest insecurities to God

Asks for confirmation

Miracles are the radical kindness of God on display.

Sense of peace

The Spirit clothes Gideon.

The Spirit didn't erase who David was.

The Spirit spoke through David—God's word was on David's tongue.

Is the prompting consistent with Scripture and the character of God?

Does the prompting cause me to love God and love others more?

Will the prompting yield the fruit of the Spirit?

Does the prompt leave me with a sense of deep peace?

Does wise, godly counsel affirm this prompting?

 30–45 minutes

GROUP DISCUSSION QUESTIONS

Leader note: *Take a few moments to review these questions, then feel free to add some of your own or whisk away any that aren't a good fit for your group. Remember, our goal isn't to cover every question but to foster meaningful discussion and experience those heart-to-heart moments that draw us closer to each other and to God as we journey together—trusting the Spirit to guide our conversations.*

1. What from today's teaching either strengthened your convictions, challenged your assumptions, or simply made you pause and think?

2. Select a few volunteers to read Judges 6:12–24. Discuss the following:

    When God called Gideon a "mighty warrior," there was a stark contrast between God's view and Gideon's self-perception. Where in your life might God see something in you that you struggle to recognize in yourself?

Gideon needed multiple confirmations before acting. On a spectrum from "immediate obedience" to "requiring many signs," where do you typically fall when sensing the Spirit's prompting?

How has this helped or hindered your spiritual journey?

3. The definition of a miracle as "the radical kindness of God on display" shifts our perspective. Share an experience of God's radical kindness that others might have missed but transformed your understanding of how the Spirit works.

    How has witnessing God's "radical kindness" in someone else's life affected your own faith journey?

4. Based on Judges 6:34, I highlight that the Spirit clothes Gideon, and this can also be interpreted as the Spirit wore Gideon like a garment. The image of the Spirit "wearing" Gideon suggests an intimate partnership where both God's power and Gideon's personality are fully present. Where have you experienced this paradox of being fully yourself while also being moved by something beyond yourself?

This clothing imagery suggests both protection and visibility. In what areas of your life do you feel "clothed" by the Spirit (protected and empowered) and in what areas do you feel spiritually exposed or vulnerable?

When you reflect on the time since this study began, how do you sense you're being contoured by the Spirit's presence, formed by the Spirit's life in you?

5. Select a few volunteers to read 1 Samuel 16:13 and 2 Samuel 23:1–2. What do these passages reveal about the presence of the Spirit in the life of David?

How might understanding that the Spirit works through our authentic selves (rather than erasing who we are) change how we view our spiritual journeys and the spiritual journeys of others?

6. **In this teaching, I tried to highlight important themes in the process of discernment from the lives of Gideon and David including:**
   - The importance of humility
   - The need to move from the *me* to the *we* with a concern for the community
   - The honesty to bring our hard questions and deep insecurities to God
   - The willingness to ask for confirmation as well as the role of peace and wise counsel

   Share a specific story of when you had to discern whether a prompting was from the Spirit. Which themes listed above were most crucial in that particular situation?

7. **I offered five practical guardrail questions whenever you're trying to discern, "Was that Holy Spirit?"**
   - Is the prompting consistent with Scripture and the character of God?
   - Does the prompting cause me to love God and love others more?
   - Will the prompting yield the fruit of the Spirit?
   - Does the prompt leave me with a sense of deep peace?
   - Does wise, godly counsel affirm this prompting?

   Looking at these five guardrail questions, share a specific example when one of these questions protected you from a misguided direction or confirmed a genuine prompting.

If you'd like to add a sixth guardrail question to this list, what would it be and why has that dimension of discernment proven important in your experience?

8 I share that, "Just because you don't see results, doesn't mean the Spirit isn't working. And remember, if you make a mistake, God's grace can still cover it. The bigger risk is being so afraid of making a mistake that you never obey at all."

When you've taken a risk in response to the Spirit and seen no visible results, what sustained your faith during that time? What did you learn that might not have been possible through immediate success?

9. If your community committed to "walking in step with the Spirit" in one specific area of shared life together, what might that look like and what tangible difference could it make in your community?

BEFORE THE NEXT SESSION...

- Tackle the three days of personal study (and optional two days to catch up and reflect) for Session 4.

- Optional: Read chapters 7–8 of *The God You Need to Know* book.

- Memorize this week's passage using the Scripture memory coloring page. As a bonus, look up the Scripture memory passage in different translations and take note of the variations.

- Try using the five guardrail questions in the discernment process and be prepared to share how it went at the next gathering.

CLOSE IN PRAYER

Consider the following prompts as you pray together for:

- Ears to hear with clarity how the Spirit is leading

- Clear confirmation in the discernment process

- Opportunities to bring healing and hope to others

But the fruit of the Spirit is love, joy, peace, forbearance, kindness, goodness, faithfulness, gentleness and self-control. Against such things there is no law. Galatians 5:22–23

SESSION FOUR

THE BEAUTY OF DISCERNMENT

PERSONAL STUDY

PERSONAL STUDY DAY 1

HOLY SPIRIT, WILL YOU CONFIRM IT?

Have you ever wondered, *Was that really God or just my imagination?* If so, congratulations! You're in great biblical company. One person who excelled in asking for confirmation was Gideon. His journey reminds us that second-guessing isn't a sign of weakness, but rather a normal, healthy part of the discernment process. Even better? God seems perfectly comfortable with our need for clarity.

Gideon asks the angel of the Lord who visits him, "If now I have found favor in your eyes, give me a sign that it is really you talking to me" (Judges 6:17).

On the continuum below, how readily do you ask the Lord for confirmation when you feel prompted to do something?

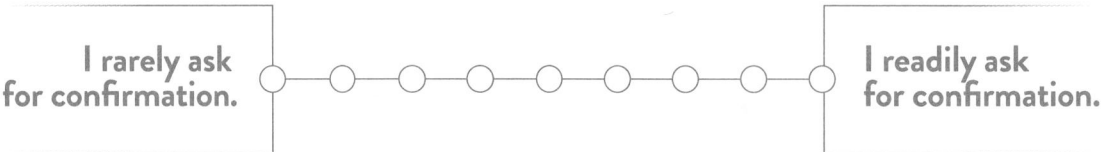

What circumstances or situations tend to prompt you to ask God for confirmation?

What holds you back from seeking confirmation at other times?

When it comes to building confidence, Gideon's journey from doubter to warrior gives us a master class on spiritual growth.

#1 CONFIRMATION: THE FIERY FEAST

When an angel of the Lord first appears, Gideon essentially says, "Prove it's really you!" Gideon prepares a generous meal for the divine visitor. When the angel touches the feast with his staff, whoosh—fire consumes everything and confirms God's presence. But that's not enough for our friend Gideon.

#2 CONFIRMATION: THE WET FLEECE

Even after the Spirit "clothes" Gideon and the troops rally, Gideon is still second-guessing and needs more assurance.

Read Judges 6:36–38. What's Gideon's unusual request? How does God respond?

#3 CONFIRMATION: THE DRY FLEECE

If you've ever received confirmation after confirmation but remained unsure, you're in good company with Gideon. The God-appointed warrior bravely asks God for one more affirmation.

Read Judges 6:39–40. How did Gideon ask for confirmation again, and what was God's response?

It's tempting for us to judge Gideon for asking for confirmation again and again, but notice that God never judges Gideon for asking.

Instead, what we see is a transformation in Gideon. If you go on to read Judges 7, you'll discover that God asks Gideon to do the unthinkable—pare his army down by more than 22,000 men to a measly 300. Gideon doesn't flinch; he merely obeys. Somewhere in the process of asking God for confirmation, Gideon encountered God in such a way that he could trust God more. And God can do the same in our lives.

Gideon wasn't alone in his desire for divine confirmation. The Bible is filled with people who asked God, "Is this really you?" Let's explore a few.

ABRAHAM'S SERVANT: DIVINE DATING CONFIRMATION

Read Genesis 24:12–19. Appointed to find a wife for Isaac, Abraham's servant prays for a confirmation. What is the request and what is the result?

JONATHAN: BATTLE PLANS CONFIRMATION

Read 1 Samuel 14:6–12. What method did Jonathan use to confirm whether God wanted him to proceed and attack the Philistines? And what is the result?

Now, sometimes people point to the example of Zechariah, the husband of Elizabeth, asking for a sign regarding the birth of his son, John the Baptist, as a reason not to ask God for confirmation. But this story differs from the others in several significant ways.

Read Luke 1:5–19. What does the angel promise, and how does Zechariah respond?

Read Luke 1:20. Why does the angel say Zechariah will become mute?

At first glance, this can be puzzling because previous servants, like Abraham's servant and Gideon, also asked for confirmation and didn't become mute.

Here's why Zechariah's situation was different:
- He received a direct, in-person message from an angel while serving in the temple—pretty hard to misinterpret.
- His question wasn't seeking confirmation but expressing doubt about whether God *could* do what was promised.
- His temporary muteness wasn't a punishment—it became a beautiful gift and sign itself.

After the months of quiet reflection—a blessed opportunity to pay close attention to all God was doing—Zechariah is transformed.

Read Luke 1:62–66. How did Zechariah respond when his voice returned, and how did this glorify God?

Even Jesus' closest followers sought confirmation of his presence and guidance.

PETER'S WALKING ON WATER CONFIRMATION

Read Matthew 14:22–29. What confirmation does Peter ask for from Jesus? How does Jesus respond?

THOMAS'S TOUCHING THE SCARS CONFIRMATION

Read John 20:24–29. How does Thomas ask for confirmation? What is Jesus' response?

THE DISCIPLES' SELECTION CONFIRMATION

Read Acts 1:21–26. When it comes time to replace Judas, the disciples seek confirmation. What do they use to request confirmation? How does the Lord respond?

Reflecting on all these biblical examples, we can see that asking for confirmation isn't a sign of weak faith—it's often a step toward deeper trust. So we shouldn't hesitate to ask the Holy Spirit to provide confirmation on whatever we're being prompted or nudged to do or leave undone.

How might you incorporate asking for confirmation in your spiritual journey going forward?

Where do you most need confirmation right now? Write your response as a prayer in the space below.

May you walk forward with both the courage to ask and the patience to wait for God's confirming voice. Like Gideon, may your requests for signs not be the end of your faith journey but the beginning of an ever-deepening trust.

Remember that the God who parted seas, sent fire from heaven, and raised Christ from the dead is the same God who delights in making his will clear to you—not because you've earned it but because you are deeply loved. The next time you find yourself asking, "Is that really you, God?" know that you're in the very best company.

PERSONAL STUDY DAY 2

HOLY SPIRIT, IS THIS REALLY YOU?

Have you ever stood at a spiritual crossroads, wondering which path to take? Or perhaps you've heard that still, small voice and wondered, *Is this really the Holy Spirit speaking to me?*

If so, you're not alone. Even the most faith-filled believers need help discerning which promptings are truly from God. Think of these five guardrail questions as your spiritual GPS—designed not to restrict your journey but to keep you safely on the path of God's best for your life.

Each question is deeply rooted in Scripture and the character of God. As you practice using them, they'll become second nature, helping you move from uncertainty to confidence in following the Spirit's lead.

GUARDRAIL QUESTION

01 Is the prompting consistant with Scripture and the character of God? ◯ yes ◯ no

This is the gold-standard question—your first and foremost filter. If something is from the Spirit, it will align with Scripture. If it doesn't, it's time to chuck it far out back.

The Bible consistently reveals God's character, so whatever the Holy Spirit prompts will harmonize with who God is and who he's calling us to be as followers of Jesus.

What does each passage below reveal about the role the Bible plays in our spiritual journeys and the discernment process? Fill in the chart.

SCRIPTURE GUIDE FOR DISCERNMENT

Scripture	Key Theme	What This Reveals About Discernment	My Response
Psalm 119:105	Scripture as a guiding light		
John 17:17	Truth and sanctification		
Hebrews 4:12	The living, active power of God's Word		

Session 4 | The Beauty of Discernment

In the discernment process, Scripture keeps us humble—one of the shared characteristics of Gideon and David that we've explored. The Bible keeps us open to correction and confirmation while inviting us into deeper conversation with the Spirit.

GUARDRAIL QUESTION

02 Does the prompting cause me to love God and love others more?

○ yes ○ no

One of the markers of Holy Spirit's promptings is that they will cause you to love God or others more . . . *and probably both.*

The Spirit's voice will gently pull you away from self-centered, self-sabotaging, or self-indulgent focus and guide you toward sacrificial acts of kindness and love centered around loving God and others. The Spirit moves us from "me" to "we."

What does each passage on the next page reveal about the significance of loving God and others in our responses?

Fill in the chart.

	LOVING GOD AND OTHERS		
Scripture	Key Theme	What This Reveals About Loving God	How This Shapes My Loving Others
Deuteronomy 6:4–6	The Shema: Loving God with all we are		
Matthew 22:37–40	The greatest commandments		
John 15:13	The ultimate demonstration of love		

How can you be more attentive to loving God and others as you discern the Spirit's guidance?

GUARDRAIL QUESTION

03   Will the prompting yield the fruit of the Spirit?   ◯ ◯
                                                                                                                          yes no

One of the hallmarks of the Spirit's work in our lives is the fruit of the Spirit. If what you've heard is from Holy Spirit, then your obedience will produce good fruit in your life. And if it doesn't, there's a good chance it's not from the Holy Spirit.

Read Galatians 5:22–23. Draw a simple fruit tree below and label each with a facet of the fruit.

Have you ever thought you should do something in response to the Spirit that didn't yield this fruitfulness? If so, what was the result?

Why is looking for the Spirit's fruitful yield so important in the discernment process?

GUARDRAIL QUESTION

04   Does the prompt leave me with a sense of deep peace? ◯ ◯
　　　　　　　　　　　　　　　　　　　　　　　　　　　　　yes   no

Remember our friend Gideon? After the encounter with the angel, what did the Lord give Gideon? Peace.

If a prompting leaves you spinning in anxiety, overwhelmed by fear, or makes you feel icky, it's *likely* not from the Spirit.

Jesus is called the Prince of Peace for good reason. Peace is one of the fruits of the Spirit, and that deep, settled peace is often a marker of the Spirit's authentic voice. We even explored how the Holy Spirit gives us peace in Day 2 of Session 2.

> And the **peace** of God, which transcends all understanding, will **guard** your hearts and your minds in Christ Jesus.
> Philippians 4:7 (emphasis added)

Reflecting on the passage above, how can you be more attentive to the role of peace in staying in step with the Spirit?

Check all that apply.

- ○ Creating regular quiet moments to experience God's peace
- ○ Noticing when worry or anxiety is replacing God's peace in your heart
- ○ Using peace as a spiritual barometer for decision-making
- ○ Intentionally asking for God's peace to guard your heart and mind
- ○ Studying biblical examples of peace amid difficult circumstances
- ○ Journaling or recounting moments when you've experienced supernatural peace
- ○ Practicing gratitude to cultivate a peaceful heart
- ○ Other: _____

GUARDRAIL QUESTION

05   Does wise, godly counsel affirm this prompting?   ○ ○
                                                       yes no

Community plays such a crucial role in the discernment process. There's nothing better than being part of a beautiful Christ-centered group of believers. What joy there is in building rich friendships with those who have been walking with Jesus for longer than you—maybe even ten or twenty or thirty years. What a gift to have people to go to and who will listen to you, pray with you, and help you discern.

What do the following passages reveal about the importance of community? Fill in the chart below.

Scripture	What the Passage Reveals About Community
Ecclesiastes 4:9	
Proverbs 27:17	
Matthew 18:20	
James 5:16	

Who are the people in your life you go to for wisdom in the discernment process?

Would it be helpful to have more of these people in your life? If so, what can you do to intentionally grow those relationships?

Remember that any prompting of the Spirit is an invitation to a conversation—to pray and reflect, to search the Scriptures and grow. The Spirit speaks not just for information but for transformation, such that you become more like Jesus.

Consider a recent decision or prompting you've experienced. In the space below, write a brief description of the situation.

Now, which guardrail question proved most helpful in this specific situation? Why?

Which guardrail question was most challenging to apply? What made it difficult?

Beyond these five guardrail questions, what additional discernment practice might be helpful in your specific context or life season?

May these guardrails not restrict your journey but give you the confidence to move forward with bold faith, knowing you're traveling the path the Spirit has laid before you.

PERSONAL STUDY DAY 3

HOLY SPIRIT, SHOULD I SAY THIS?

Have you ever felt that gentle nudge to say something encouraging to a stranger? Or perhaps experienced words of wisdom tumbling from your lips that seemed wiser than your usual thoughts? This is the beautiful mystery of Spirit-led speech—where your voice becomes a vessel for divine life and hope.

As followers of Jesus, we've received the remarkable gift of the Holy Spirit—the same Spirit who inspired David's psalms and has been delivering words of life since creation's dawn. Every conversation holds potential for us to:

- Speak life into weary souls.
- Fortify discouraged hearts.
- Reveal gifts in others they can't yet see in themselves.
- Transform the echoes of death into a resurrection roar.

But how do we know when it's truly the Spirit prompting our words versus our own thoughts, emotions, or agendas? Let's explore together.

One simple but profound way to align our speech with the Spirit is to soak in Scripture—the greatest love letter ever written. When we create space for God's words to take root in our hearts, they unleash transformative power in our attitudes, actions, and especially our speech.

How has Scripture changed the way you speak to or about others? Share a specific example if you can.

If you've ever felt the Spirit nudging you to say something to someone, you may have wrestled with the same questions I do:

Is this truly from the Spirit?
When should I speak these words?
How should I approach this person?
What tone should I use?

Even when we've applied our guardrail questions and determined our words align with God's heart, the discernment process has just begun. We must also examine our hearts to ensure that our delivery and tone reflect God's compassion and love.

If we're uncertain in any way—about the person we're speaking to, the timing of our words, or even the words themselves—it's best to take time to pray and wait. It's wiser to err on the side of silence paired with extended prayer than to speak rashly.

Read Proverbs 12:18. What does this reveal about reckless speech?

What's the fruit of using our words wisely?

The book of Job contains a fascinating character study in how not to speak on God's behalf. Job, a man of great wealth and virtue, lost almost everything in a series of devastating blows, leaving him grieving in profound silence (Job 1–2).

As his suffering deepened, his friends arrived, but instead of offering comfort they condemned him, accusing him of hidden sin and urging him to repent. Despite the overwhelming suffering and the apparent absence of justice, Job still holds on to his faith. Job says of God:

> "In his hand is the life of every creature
> and the **breath** [ruach] of all mankind."
> Job 12:10 (emphasis added)

Job knows that his next breath, all of creation's next breath, is dependent on God. The friends who surround Job in his loss have a lot to learn. One of these friends, Elihu, finds common ground with Job when he says:

> "The **Spirit** [*ruach*] of God has made me;
> the **breath** [*nishmat*] of the Almighty gives me life."
>
> Job 33:4 (emphasis added)

Job sees the breath of God everywhere, in all of creation. Job takes the perspective of the "we," whereas Elihu is focused on the "me": "God has *made me* . . . the Almighty *gives me*." It's a subtle difference but one that becomes even more apparent when Elihu claims to speak by the Spirit's compulsion.

Read Job 32:1–5. What is Elihu's attitude toward Job and his friends?

Read Job 32:6–14. What is the tone of Elihu's words?

Despite the anger evident in his heart, Elihu makes an extraordinary claim about his speech:

> "I too will have my say;
> I too will tell what I know.
> For I am full of words,
> and the **spirit** [*ruach*] within me compels me;
> inside I am like bottled-up wine,
> like new wineskins ready to burst.
> I must speak and find relief;
> I must open my lips and reply."
>
> Job 32:17–20 (emphasis added)

Though Elihu has something to say, it's not compelled by the Spirit. As my friend, scholar Jack Levison, explains in *A Boundless God*:

> His assumption is mistaken; he thinks the need to speak
> is the product of God's spirit-breath within rather than
> his own rash restlessness. He thinks that an excess of energy,
> a burst of words, equals a surplus of the spirit and sufficient wisdom....
> What he says does not arise from discipline, from learning, from study;
> what he says arises from his own impatience and impetuosity.[5]

When have you confused your own urgency to speak with the Spirit's prompting? What was the result?

While Elihu's ongoing speeches are not specifically rebuked by God at the end of Job, the rashness of his speech fueled by anger was not compelled by the Spirit as he claimed. Elihu highlights the importance of discernment long before we say something to someone else. (A lesson I've had to learn the hard way!) It reminds us of the importance of humility.

Words given by the Spirit are meant to be gifts, and gift-givers don't demand, "This is your gift, and you must like it." Instead, we should approach others with humble hearts that honor them above ourselves.

When sharing what you believe the Spirit has prompted, consider gentle framing like:

- "This may be of no use to you at all, but I just sense in my heart that . . ."
- "I've been praying for you, and this might not mean anything, but this came to mind . . ."
- "I'm not sure if this will resonate, but I felt I should share . . ."

This approach acknowledges that we sense the Spirit imperfectly, creating space for both giver and receiver to discern together.

What words or phrases might help you deliver Spirit-prompted messages with humility?

One of the best guides for discerning Spirit-led speech is found in 1 Corinthians 13—the famous "love chapter." This passage follows directly after

Paul's teaching on spiritual gifts in 1 Corinthians 12, suggesting that love is the ultimate filter for all spiritual expressions, including speech.

Read 1 Corinthians 13:1–3. What spiritual gifts and acts are listed in this passage?

What becomes of each of these gifts or acts apart from love?

First Corinthians 13 becomes a kind of colander that we can sift our words through to see what, if anything, remains.

> If your words are always patient, always kind, always protecting, always hoping, always persevering, you can have a measure of confidence the Spirit is at work. If your words are devoid of arrogance and pride, dishonor and self-centeredness, anger and grudges, the Spirit may be operating through them. If your words refuse to delight in evil and instead rejoice with truth, there could be a touch of the Spirit in what you say. And if your words are marked by faith, hope, and love most of all, the Spirit just might be resting on your lips. Spirit-infused words have a shelf life beyond all the ordinary syllables we speak.
>
> from *The God You Need to Know* p. 104

If you've sensed the Holy Spirit nudging you to say something—whether at work, at church, or to family or friends—use the following guide as a prayerful, reflective resource for discernment.

THE LOVE FILTER
Based on 1 Corinthians 13, consider whether your words are:

Quality	Yes	No	Not Sure
Patient	○	○	○
Kind	○	○	○
Free from envy	○	○	○
Not boastful	○	○	○
Not proud	○	○	○
Not dishonoring	○	○	○
Not self-seeking	○	○	○
Not easily angered	○	○	○
Keeping no record of wrongs	○	○	○
Not delighting in evil	○	○	○
Rejoicing in truth	○	○	○
Protecting	○	○	○
Trusting	○	○	○
Hoping	○	○	○
Persevering	○	○	○

Now, let's put this into practice. Think of a situation where you believe the Spirit might be prompting you to speak words of life, encouragement, correction, or guidance to someone.

Describe the situation.

What specific words do you feel prompted to share?

How will you approach this conversation with humility?

After filtering these words through 1 Corinthians 13, do you still believe this is from the Spirit? Why or why not?

Always remember that Spirit-led words have a shelf life far beyond ordinary syllables. They echo into eternity.

PERSONAL STUDY CATCH-UP DAYS 4 & 5

HOLY SPIRIT, TEACH ME MORE

Use these extra days to go back and complete any of the reflection questions or activities from the previous days this week that you weren't able to finish. Make note of any insights you've had and make a list of any stories you'd like to share with your group the next time you gather.

OPTIONAL:

Spend the next two days reading chapters 7–8 of the book *The God You Need to Know*. Use the space below to note anything in the chapters that stands out to you or encourages your heart.

"Beyond the veil of impossibility, the Spirit breathes life into barren places and resurrects hope from the ashes. Even in the darkest nights, the work of *ruach* continues, weaving threads of redemption into the fabric of existence. Not even death can halt the purposes of God."

FROM *THE GOD YOU NEED TO KNOW*
p. 116

SESSION FIVE

THE SPIRIT'S DELIGHTFUL SURPRISES

GROUP STUDY

SCHEDULE

OPTIONAL BEFORE GROUP MEETING	Read chapters 7–8 in *The God You Need to Know* book.
DURING GROUP MEETING	Watch teaching video for Session 5. Group discussion will follow, pages 176–181.
PERSONAL STUDY DAY 1	Study guide pages 183–189
PERSONAL STUDY DAY 2	Study guide pages 190–193
PERSONAL STUDY DAY 3	Study guide pages 194–197
PERSONAL STUDY CATCH-UP DAYS 4 & 5	Complete any unfinished Personal Study activities. Optional: Read chapters 9–10 in *The God You Need to Know* book.

 5–10 minutes

OPENING GROUP DISCUSSION

Last week, we explored the five guardrail questions for spiritual discernment:

1. Is the prompting consistent with Scripture and the character of God?
2. Does the prompting cause me to love God and love others more?
3. Will the prompting yield the fruit of the Spirit?
4. Does the prompt leave me with a sense of deep peace?
5. Does wise, godly counsel affirm this prompting?

> Did you have an opportunity to use any of these questions in your daily life this past week? If so, what was that experience like for you?

 23 minutes

SESSION 5 VIDEO

Leader, stream the video or play the DVD.

> **SCRIPTURE COVERED IN THIS TEACHING SESSION:**
> Ezekiel 2:1–8; 37:3–10; Romans 8:11

VIDEO NOTES

As you watch, use the outline to help you follow along and take notes on anything that stands out to you.

The phrase "Son of man" describes Ezekiel and Jesus.

Lifting up of Ezekiel

Valley of dry bones

The work of the Spirit didn't happen in an instant, but in a divinely orchestrated sequence.

Just because you don't see something happening doesn't mean the Spirit isn't working.

"Write to him."

Hot breath

You can't rush a resurrection.

Listen for the sacred echoes.

Remember, small obedience matters.

Look for the surprise and delight of the Spirit.

 30–45 minutes

GROUP DISCUSSION QUESTIONS

Leader note: *Take a few moments to review these questions, then feel free to add some of your own or whisk away any that aren't a good fit for your group. Remember, our goal isn't to cover every question but to foster meaningful discussion and experience those heart-to-heart moments that draw us closer to each other and to God as we journey together—trusting the Spirit to guide our conversations.*

1. As we process this fifth session together, what did you find most impactful—either as encouragement, a challenge to your thinking, or simply as a memorable insight?

2. Take turns reading Ezekiel 2:1–8. Discuss the following:

    What specific challenges does the Spirit warn Ezekiel he'll face despite his faithful obedience? What strikes you about God's honesty with Ezekiel?

Describe a specific moment when you clearly followed the Spirit's guidance and found yourself facing unexpected resistance or difficulty. What surprised you most about that experience?

How does our culture's emphasis on "blessing" sometimes conflict with the biblical reality of Spirit-led hardship?

Looking back on that challenging season of obedience, what specific growth or transformation occurred in you that likely wouldn't have happened through an easier path?

3. **Select a few volunteers to read Ezekiel 37:3–10 and Romans 8:11. Discuss the following:**

    What "valley of dry bones" in your life needs the Spirit's breath of life?

    It's sometimes easier to believe in resurrection power for someone else than for ourselves. Where do you find yourself saying, "Yes, but not for me"?

What makes those particular areas difficult to surrender to the Spirit's reviving work?

4. I share the struggle, "Often we want the Spirit of the Living God to work in the way we expect, using the means we expect, in the sequence we expect, on the timetable we expect. Yet this scene in Ezekiel reminds us that Holy Spirit often works in unexpected ways—ways that leave us in spaces and places of waiting."

   The Spirit rarely follows our preferred schedules or methods. What situation in your life has lingered in the "waiting room" far longer than you expected? How has your attitude toward God evolved during this extended waiting?

   In Ezekiel's vision, restoration came in stages—first tendons, then flesh, then skin, and finally breath. How does viewing the Spirit's restoration as a process change your perspective on current challenges?

5. Share a story of "impossible restoration"—a relationship, situation, or personal struggle where you witnessed the Spirit bring life in a way that seemed humanly impossible at the time.

   How does revisiting "resurrection stories" build resilience for your current challenges?

6. The Spirit often speaks through persistent nudges like Sasha's "Write to him!" experience. What recurring thought might be the Spirit's invitation rather than your own idea?

   What Spirit-prompted action remains undone? What's one small step toward obedience?

7. "Sacred echoes" are when the same message comes through multiple channels—perhaps a sermon, then a friend's comment, then a passage in your reading. Share an example of when you experienced this convergence of prompting from seemingly unrelated sources.

8. **Sometimes when the prompting of the Holy Spirit feels small, it's easy to dismiss and think, *That won't make any difference*. In part, because we assume the size of the ask or task is directly correlated to the size of the impact. Yet often it's the simplest acts of obedience that have the biggest eternal consequences.**

   Describe a time when what seemed like a small act of obedience to the Spirit led to surprising or disproportionate impact. What did this teach you about your ability to discern significance?

9. **Many of us know a little bit about the Holy Spirit's power and presence, but perhaps less about the Spirit's delight and joy. In what ways have you discovered the Holy Spirit as playful, joyful, or surprising that have expanded your understanding of God's character?**

BEFORE THE NEXT SESSION...

- Tackle the three days of personal study (and optional two days to catch up and reflect) for Session 5.

- Optional: Read chapters 9–10 of *The God You Need to Know* book.

- Memorize this week's passage using the Scripture memory coloring page. As a bonus, look up the Scripture memory passage in different translations and take note of the variations.

- Try the three practices from this session and be prepared to share how it went at the next gathering.

- **Ask members to bring something for the next session's Opening Group Activity—it's my favorite one!** (See page 201 for instructions.)

CLOSE IN PRAYER

Consider the following prompts as you pray together for:

- Ears to hear your sacred echoes
- Opportunities to practice small obedience
- Eyes to see the surprise and delight of the Spirit

This is what the Sovereign Lord says to these bones: I will make breath enter you, and you will come to life. I will attach tendons to you and make flesh come upon you and cover you with skin; I will put breath in you, and you will come to life. Then you will know that I am the Lord.

Ezekiel 37:5–6

SESSION FIVE

THE SPIRIT'S DELIGHTFUL SURPRISES

PERSONAL STUDY

PERSONAL STUDY DAY 1

HOLY SPIRIT, HELP ME RECOGNIZE THE SACRED ECHOES

Have you ever noticed how some messages seem to follow you everywhere? The same theme appears in your morning devotional, then a friend mentions it over coffee, then it shows up in a song on your drive home. Coincidence? Perhaps. But what if these "echoes" are actually sacred reverberations—divine repetitions designed to capture your attention?

While a single whisper of the Spirit might leave us uncertain, the repetitive nature of a sacred echo gives us confidence that the Spirit really is prompting, guiding, or leading us. These echoes invite us to pay attention and to consider prayerfully how the Spirit is working not just in our lives but in those around us. Each echo is an invitation to spiritual transformation and growth.

One of the most powerful examples of sacred echoes appears in the life of the prophet Elijah. After his mountaintop victory over the prophets of Baal in 1 Kings 18, Elijah finds himself on the run—a burned-out, exhausted prophet ready to throw in the towel.

Read 1 Kings 19:1–8. How does Elijah respond to hitting such a low point in his life?

How does God respond to Elijah in his moment of despair? What hope does this give you for how God will respond to you in your low points?

Read 1 Kings 19:9. What does God ask Elijah? Why does God ask Elijah a question when he already knows the answer?

Elijah doesn't hold back in his response. He brings his toughest questions and greatest frustrations directly to God.

> "I have been very zealous for the Lord God Almighty.
> The Israelites have rejected your covenant, torn down your altars,
> and put your prophets to death with the sword.
> I am the only one left, and now they are trying to kill me too."
> 1 Kings 19:10

The prophet's life is on the line, yet God doesn't address any of his concerns. Instead, God instructs Elijah to do something unusual: Go stand on the mountain and wait. I can only imagine Elijah's internal monologue as he huffed across the rocky terrain.

The next couple verses of 1 Kings 19 describe the extraordinary encounter Elijah experiences atop the mountain. Standing thousands of feet above sea level, Elijah feels the wind pick up. Before he can process what's happening, hurricane-force winds rip apart the surrounding rocks. Then, without warning, the wind stops. Next comes a rumbling beneath his feet—an earthquake shaking the ground. When the trembling subsides, Elijah looks around cautiously. What's next? Fire erupts all around him, smoke filling the air as he tries to protect himself.

And then . . . silence. In this quiet moment, Elijah experiences what he has been waiting for: God finally draws near to the worn-out prophet in the gentle sound of a whisper.

Read 1 Kings 19:11–13. What does this text reveal? Fill in the blanks below:

The Lord was not in the _____.

The Lord was not in the _____.

The Lord was not in the _____.

Yet God used a chain of natural—no, supernatural—events to prepare Elijah for an encounter with himself. The repeated display of power didn't just get Elijah's attention—it kept it.

God then asks Elijah the *exact* same question from verse 9: "What are you doing here, Elijah?" The prophet responds:

"I have been very zealous for the LORD God Almighty. The Israelites have rejected your covenant, torn down your altars, and put your prophets to death with the sword. I am the only one left, and now they are trying to kill me too."

1 Kings 19:14

What similarities do you see between Elijah's response to God in verses 10 and 14?

Elijah offers a familiar answer, but this time God responds differently. He provides Elijah with specific instruction, encouragement, and even companionship.

Read 1 Kings 19:15–18. How does God respond to Elijah?

Our outrageously generous God provides for this torn-up prophet:

Physically with food
Emotionally with friendship
Relationally with a partner in ministry (Elisha)
Spiritually with encouragement

God echoes life back into the prophet. This passage reveals something transformative: Neither the wind, earthquake, nor fire happened apart from God's knowledge or permission. In fact, God used these repeated demonstrations to prepare Elijah for a divine encounter.

Like an echo, God often uses repetitive events and themes in our daily lives to get our attention and draw us closer to himself. Instead of just listening for God's whisper, we can recognize these *sacred echoes*—those moments when the Spirit speaks the same message to our hearts again and again.

I call them sacred echoes because I've noticed that throughout my relationships, daily life, and study that the same scripturally sound idea or phrase or word will keep reappearing until I can no longer avoid its presence. Sometimes it's mere coincidence, but often there's something more.

What does the Spirit often use to get your attention? Circle any that apply.

Scripture – A verse pops from the Bible and speaks directly into what you're facing.

Prayer – In quiet moments, you feel a prompting, peace, or conviction.

Other People – Friends, family, co-workers, or even strangers say something timely or significant.

Circumstances – Hardships or unexpected provisions awaken you to the nearness of God.

Creation – A sunset, the rumble of thunder, or a moss-lined stream reminds you of the Spirit's presence.

Music – A song, hymn, or lyrics carry a personal, timely message that resonates deeply.

Dreams – The Spirit may use a dream as a prayer prompt to reveal something specific.

Inner Promptings – A still, small voice or deep sense of knowing nudges you to action.

Open or Closed Doors – Opportunities that emerge or evaporate suddenly shift the path you're on.

Other: _____

Has the Spirit ever spoken a sacred echo to you? If so, describe the experience.

How can you become more attentive to the sacred echoes in your life?

More and more, I find I need these sacred echoes—the persistent voice of God's Spirit—almost as if my life depends on it. They remind me the Spirit has not departed, is steadfast, and has not given up on me. As I grow older, I need more certainty—not less—in responding to the Spirit's promptings.

Faith isn't just moving forward when the Spirit seems distant. Sometimes faith is waiting until the Spirit draws near before taking the first step.

PERSONAL STUDY DAY 2

HOLY SPIRIT, HELP ME WAIT WELL

Waiting on God is one of the most challenging aspects of faith. Whether it's waiting for a job, a relationship, healing, or direction, delays can be frustrating and even discouraging. However, Scripture teaches that waiting on the Lord is not passive—it is an active, faith-filled process where the Holy Spirit works behind the scenes to bring about God's work at the appointed time.

One of the most dramatic waiting stories belongs to Joseph, who spent years in an Egyptian prison despite his innocence.

Read Genesis 39:20–23. How was the Lord with Joseph while he waited in prison?

What does this reveal about what the Lord can do in our seasons of waiting?

Genesis 40 tells of Joseph interpreting the dreams of Pharaoh's imprisoned cupbearer and baker. Joseph acknowledged that these interpretations come from God, and the dreams came true exactly as he predicted. The cupbearer was restored to his position, and the baker was executed, just as Joseph had foreseen. But the cupbearer forgot Joseph, leaving him in prison for two more years.

What does it look like for you to trust God in seasons of waiting?

At the right moment, the Spirit gave Joseph wisdom to interpret Pharaoh's troubling dreams, leading to an astonishing promotion.

Read Genesis 41:38–41. What does Joseph's story teach us about the Spirit's timing versus our own expectations?

How can we prepare ourselves spiritually and mentally while waiting for the Spirit to work in our own lives, just as Joseph did?

The principle of the Spirit working in waiting appears also in the life of Othniel, the first judge of Israel, who was chosen by God to deliver the people from oppression.

Read Judges 3:7–9. What was the result of the Israelites doing evil in the sight of the Lord?

We might read this passage quickly and think God brought Caleb's younger brother, Othniel, to them overnight. But notice the Scripture says God "raised up for them," suggesting this happened over time, not instantly.

Read Judges 3:10–11. At the appointed time, what does the Holy Spirit do?

What is the result of the Spirit of the Lord in Othniel's life and for the community of Israelites?

How can you rely on the Holy Spirit in times of waiting and live faithfully and expectantly for the Spirit's provision and guidance?

PERSONAL STUDY DAY 3

HOLY SPIRIT, SURPRISE AND DELIGHT ME WITH YOUR PRESENCE

The Holy Spirit is always present, often surprising us and delighting us in ways that lead to deeper intimacy with God. Each day offers opportunities to be surprised by the Spirit's presence, to delight in the Spirit's work, and to respond with worship and thanksgiving.

One person who I suspect was overwhelmed by the surprise and delight of the Spirit is Simeon. Long before we meet Simeon, the Holy Spirit has whispered in his ear that he will see the Messiah before he dies (Luke 2:26). Simeon, whose name means "one who hears," was well known throughout his community for being righteous and devout.

Read Luke 2:25–26. What does this passage reveal about the work of the Spirit in Simeon's life?

Read Luke 2:27–33. What does the Spirit prompt Simeon to do and what is the result?

How does Simeon express his surprise, delight, and joy in this passage?

Simeon holds the delight of God in his arms, and I can imagine him grinning as the baby squirms, legs kicking in the air. All this man's deepest longings and desires materialize in this miniature package of humanity. Simeon will forever be a witness that God keeps his promises. Simeon blesses Joseph. Simeon blesses Mary. Then, Simeon speaks prophetic, soul-penetrating words to the young mom.

Read Luke 2:33–35. What does Simeon say to Mary?

I often wonder how many times Mary, who stored meaningful moments in her heart, returned to those words for encouragement, for strength, for understanding. She no doubt carried these words with her, and at times, the words most likely carried her—all because the Spirit worked in and through the life of Simeon.

How do you experience the Spirit's goodness in your everyday life, and what specific gifts or blessings have you received through the Spirit's work?

What are some practical ways to recognize and celebrate the Spirit's presence and work in your everyday life?

Read Romans 14:17. What is the relationship between righteousness, peace, and joy in this passage?

How does the Holy Spirit contribute to the joy we experience in God's presence?

This joy and delight are not fleeting or dependent on circumstances but are grounded in our relationship with God, the work of the Holy Spirit, and our hope in eternity. We can experience a deep, lasting joy that sustains us through all of life's ups and downs.

How can you incorporate worship and gratitude for the Holy Spirit into your daily routines?

How can you cultivate a lifestyle that allows you to delight in the Holy Spirit every day?

As you continue to become more attentive to the Spirit, may you find yourself increasingly aware of the divine choreography happening all around you—and within you—every single day.

PERSONAL STUDY CATCH-UP DAYS 4 & 5

HOLY SPIRIT, TEACH ME MORE

Use these extra days to go back and complete any of the reflection questions or activities from the previous days this week that you weren't able to finish. Make note of any insights you've had and make a list of any stories you'd like to share with your group the next time you gather.

> **OPTIONAL:**
>
> Spend the next two days reading chapters 9–10 of the book *The God You Need to Know*. Use the space below to note anything in the chapters that stands out to you or encourages your heart.

PREPARATION FOR OUR FINAL WEEK CELEBRATION!

Bring an item that represents the Holy Spirit or something that the Holy Spirit has done in your life. Like the cover of the book and Bible study, this item can symbolically represent how the Holy Spirit has become real to you.

These will be folded into a bouquet or display for the final gathering.

If you have access, consider picking up some greenery or flowers to help build the bouquet or display.

In addition, you may want to contribute a sharable snack, some streamers, or party balloons as part of the celebration.

"When the Spirit says, 'Go!' and you obey, who knows what might happen? What role might you play in the answer to someone's answered prayer? What help might you give to someone God is rescuing from a bad situation? What person might you meet who comes to faith? What miracle might you see? What healing might you be part of? All those little prompts and nudges to *go* matter more than you realize. And through them, the Spirit works mightily."

FROM *THE GOD YOU NEED TO KNOW*
p. 158

SESSION SIX

WHEN THE SPIRIT SAYS "GO!"

GROUP STUDY

SCHEDULE

OPTIONAL BEFORE GROUP MEETING	Read chapters 9–10 in *The God You Need to Know* book.
DURING GROUP MEETING	Watch teaching video for Session 6. Group discussion will follow, pages 206–211.
PERSONAL STUDY DAY 1	Study guide pages 213–218
PERSONAL STUDY DAY 2	Study guide pages 219–223
PERSONAL STUDY DAY 3	Study guide pages 224–226
PERSONAL STUDY CATCH-UP DAYS 4 & 5	Complete any unfinished Personal Study activities. Optional: Finish reading any unread chapters in *The God You Need to Know* book.

 10–15 minutes

OPENING GROUP DISCUSSION

LET'S CELEBRATE

Arrange the items that each person brought in a bouquet or display of any sort.

Take a photo of your group's representation of Holy Spirit in each of your lives and send it to **hello@margaretfeinberg.com** so our team can see glimpses of how the Holy Spirit has been working in your life.

Discuss the following questions:

What item did you bring, and how does it represent the person or work of the Holy Spirit in your life?

Of the following three practices to stay in step with the Spirit in the last session, which did you try and how did it go?

- **Listen for the Sacred Echoes.**
- **Remember Small Obedience Matters.**
- **Look for the Surprise and Delight of the Spirit.**

 23 minutes

SESSION 6 VIDEO

Leader, stream the video or play the DVD.

SCRIPTURE COVERED IN THIS TEACHING SESSION:
Acts 2:1–11, 38–41

VIDEO NOTES

As you watch, use the outline to help you follow along and take notes on anything that stands out to you.

The Greek word for "wind" (*pneuma*) also means "breath" or "air in motion."

Fire symbolized a purifying agent and the presence of God.

They declared the magnificence, excellence, and greatness of God.

Noah, Abram, Deborah, Nathan, Amos, and many more were instructed to "Go."

Story of looking under the table

"Go moments"

Will in Cuba

Jesus, I need a Savior. I can't do this life on my own. Use my life. Forgive me. Transform me. Fill me with your Spirit. Make me like you. In Jesus' name. Amen.

 30–45 minutes

GROUP DISCUSSION QUESTIONS

Leader note: *Take a few moments to review these questions, then feel free to add some of your own or whisk away any that aren't a good fit for your group. Remember, our goal isn't to cover every question but to foster meaningful discussion and experience those heart-to-heart moments that draw us closer to each other and to God as we journey together—trusting the Spirit to guide our conversations.*

1. What challenged, inspired, or stood out to you about this final session?

2. I share the story of the wealthy newspaper publisher who searched far and wide for a painting, not realizing that it had been sitting in his warehouse all along—always present but not delighted in. We often search for what we already possess.

   Throughout this Bible study you've been given an invitation and opportunities to discover the Holy Spirit's presence and delight in the Spirit's nearness and work in your life.

How has this study helped you "uncrate" or discover the Holy Spirit in your life?

3. Invite a few participants to read Acts 2:1–11. Then revisit what you discussed in the first session's group discussion on pages 16–20.

    How does understanding the Spirit's work throughout Israel's history, as we've explored in this study, enrich your understanding of what happened at Pentecost?

4. Invite a few participants to read Acts 2:38–41. Discuss the following:

    Peter gives specific instructions in verse 38. What are they, and why do you think each element matters?

    The early believers experienced the gift of the Spirit and formed a new kind of community. What might it look like for us to live as a Spirit-filled community today?

    Have you ever been baptized? If not, would you like to be baptized?

5. I vulnerably tell the story of being prompted to go look underneath a table in a prayer room at the conference. That became a marker in my spiritual journey of the importance of responding to the nudges to "Go." The Spirit often nudges us with a simple "go," sometimes in unexpected directions. Circle any ways you've sensed the Spirit prompt you to "go" listed below.

    Go apologize.

    Go send an encouraging note.

    Go bake a casserole.

    Go visit someone in the hospital.

    Go mend a relationship.

    Go give a gift.

    Go pay someone's bill.

    Go share the love of God.

    Go volunteer after a natural disaster or crisis.

    Other: _____

Select one and briefly share what happened when you responded to that nudge. How did that experience impact how you listen for the Spirit's voice?

6. The story of Will in Cuba reminds us that the Spirit works in ways that often surprise us.

    What element of Will's story resonated with you most? Challenged you the most?

    What barriers sometimes prevent us from recognizing or believing the Spirit might work through us in similar ways?

7. Throughout our journey together, we've explored many practices to help us awaken to the Spirit's presence.

   Session 1: Marinate in Scripture
   Make Space to Listen
   Talk About the Holy Spirit with Others

   Session 2: Stay Alert to the Holy Spirit's Hovering
   Engage the Spirit Through Journaling
   Remain Curious with the Spirit

   Session 3: Breathe Prayer as Naturally as Air
   Surrender Perfectionism

   Session 4: Use the Five Guardrail Questions for Discernment

   Session 5: Listen for the Sacred Echoes
   Remember Small Obedience Matters
   Look for the Surprise and Delight of the Spirit

   Session 6: Obey the Spirit's Prompt to "Go!"

   Which one of these practices has become integrated into your daily rhythm already?

   Looking ahead, which practice do you believe the Spirit is specifically inviting you to develop further over the next three months? Why that one?

What potential obstacles might make continuing these practices difficult after our group ends? How might you navigate those challenges?

Who in your life could be a spiritual companion to help you maintain these practices beyond our study?

As we conclude our time together, complete this sentence:

"Before this study, I thought the Holy Spirit was _____
_____.

Now I understand the Spirit is _____
_____."

8. Share one specific way you plan to live differently following this study because of what you've discovered about the Spirit.

What question about the Holy Spirit are you still curious to explore further?

TO COMPLETE THIS STUDY...

- Tackle the five days of personal study (and optional two days to catch up and reflect) for Session 6.

- Optional: Complete reading any unread chapters of *The God You Need to Know* book.

- Memorize this week's passage.

- Discuss future Bible studies you might do as a group. Consider: *James: What You Do Matters*; *Revelation: Extravagant Hope*; or *Taste and See: Discovering God Among Butchers, Bakers, and Fresh Food Makers*. They're delightful—I promise!

CLOSE IN PRAYER

Consider the following prompts as you pray together for:

- Spirit-led prompts to "Go!"

- Trust even when we don't see the outcome

- Renewed joy in being part of God's kingdom

Repent and be baptized, every one of you, in the name of Jesus Christ for the forgiveness of your sins. And you will receive the gift of the Holy Spirit. The promise is for you and your children and for all who are far off—for all whom the Lord our God will call. **Acts 2:38-39**

SESSION SIX

WHEN THE SPIRIT SAYS "GO!"

PERSONAL STUDY

PERSONAL STUDY DAY 1

HOLY SPIRIT, WHERE ARE YOU ASKING ME TO GO?

Throughout Scripture we see God repeatedly calling people to "go." This unassuming command becomes the moment ordinary lives pivot toward extraordinary purposes, when shepherds become kings, farmers become prophets, and the reluctant become the resolute. While the Holy Spirit isn't necessarily the one to say "go" in the following examples, we can learn much from the "go moments."

DEBORAH

In a turbulent time, Deborah emerged as the only female judge in Scripture. Holding court beneath her namesake palm tree, this prophetess guided Israel for forty years.

Read Judges 4:4–9. In verse 6, Deborah delivers a Spirit-inspired "Go" command to Barak. What specifically does she tell him to do?

What was Barak's response to this "Go" command, and what does it reveal about his confidence in either God's message or his own leadership abilities?

Have you ever sensed God calling you to step out, but felt you needed someone to "go with you" as Barak did? What happened?

ISAIAH

Among the prophets, Isaiah is known for his longevity. His ministry spanned approximately sixty years and through the reigns of four kings of Judah.

Read Isaiah 6:1–9. What does the Lord ask Isaiah in verse 8? How does Isaiah respond?

Look up these additional "Go" commands to Isaiah. What was he told to do in each?

Have you ever said, "Send me!" before knowing the details of what God was asking? If so, what happened?

JEREMIAH

For forty years, Jeremiah stood firm while his world crumbled. As Jerusalem's fall approached, his public tears flowed so freely he became known as "the weeping prophet." What stunning courage to love so deeply the very people who scorned his message. Look up the following passages and note what Jeremiah was told to go do.

Read Jeremiah 1:4–10. How did Jeremiah respond when called? How did God respond to Jeremiah's objection?

AMOS

Amos was a shepherd long before he received a call from God to prophesy to the northern kingdom of Israel around 760–750 BC. His direct, unpolished style reflected his rural background. Amos delivered God's message against social injustices, empty religious rituals, and exploitation of the poor, bringing God's message of justice from the pastures to the palaces.

Read Amos 7:12–15. What opposition did Amos face when following God's command to "Go"?

When have you felt led by God into something uncomfortable or difficult? How did you respond?

Reflecting on these biblical examples, what patterns do you notice? Check all that apply.

○ The "go" often came to ordinary people from diverse backgrounds.

○ Some recipients felt inadequate or unqualified at first.

○ The commands often required courage to fulfill.

○ God addressed fears and objections with promises of his presence.

○ Other: _____

Which of these biblical figures' stories resonates most with your own spiritual journey? Why?

Your "go" may not sound exactly like these women and men, but it's no less significant in God's ongoing work. The question isn't whether opportunities to "go" will come, but whether we'll move when prompted. Not whether God can work through us, but whether we'll make ourselves available. Are you ready to respond to where the Spirit is asking you to go?

PERSONAL STUDY DAY 2

HOLY SPIRIT, I WANT TO GO!

It's not just the prophets who receive and dispense the command to "go." Throughout Scripture, we find the Trinity unleashing divine power, presence, and purposes through this little word.

In your own life, how comfortable are you with uncertainty when following God's leading? Mark your response on the continuum below.

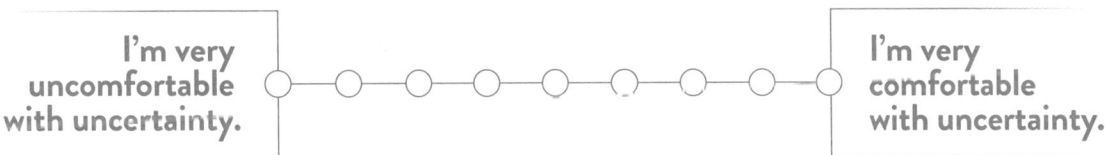

What makes stepping into uncertainty easier or harder for you?

Jesus culminated his earthly ministry with the ultimate "Go" command in Matthew 28:19–20.

Read Matthew 28:19–20 and fill in the blanks.

"Therefore _____ and make _____ of all _____, _____ them in the name of the _____ and of the _____ and of the _____ _____, and _____ them to _____ everything I have commanded you. And surely I am _____ _____ always, to the very end of the _____."

How are you currently participating in the Great Commission? Check all that apply.

○ Praying for those who don't know Jesus yet

○ Building relationships with those who don't know Jesus yet

○ Sharing my faith story when opportunities arise

○ Supporting outreach financially

○ Learning about other cultures and contexts

○ Teaching others to follow Jesus

○ Stepping out of my comfort zone to reach new people

○ Other: _____

Group these Great Commission activities under "Going" or "Staying."

Making disciples

Baptizing

Teaching obedience

Being Christ's witnesses

Relying on Christ's presence

Going Activites	Staying or Ongoing Activites

After Pentecost, the Holy Spirit continued issuing "Go" commands that expanded the gospel's reach.

Read Acts 8:26–40 about Philip's encounter with the Ethiopian eunuch after the Spirit told him to "Go."

How quickly did Philip respond, and what might that teach us about responding to "go moments" quickly?

How does the Spirit typically speak "Go" to you? Check all that apply.

- ◯ Through Scripture reading
- ◯ Through wise counsel from others
- ◯ Inner prompting/peace
- ◯ Dreams or visions
- ◯ During prayer
- ◯ Circumstances / open doors
- ◯ Repeated themes or messages
- ◯ Other: _____

Take a moment to ask the Spirit quietly, "Is there anywhere you're asking me to 'go' right now?" Write down any thoughts that come to mind.

Isaiah's response remains our model: "Here am I. Send me!" (Isaiah 6:8).

What typically holds you back from responding to God's "Go" commands? Check all that apply.

- ○ Fear of the unknown
- ○ Feeling inadequate or unprepared
- ○ Lack of clarity about the details
- ○ Previous disappointments
- ○ Concern about what others will think
- ○ Comfort with my current situation
- ○ Financial concerns
- ○ Other: _____

Identify one small "Go" step you can take this week in response to the Spirit's leading. Write a statement of declaration here:

PERSONAL STUDY DAY 3

HOLY SPIRIT, LEAD ME EVERY STEP OF THE WAY

Sometimes the most profound discoveries don't arrive in a single grand moment but in the slow accumulation of little awakenings. Take a few moments to page through your notes and responses throughout this study guide. Place a star by those that shimmer with particular significance for you. The Holy Spirit often speaks through what lingers, what returns to mind, and what refuses to be forgotten.

As you've been studying the Holy Spirit, what are three of the most important truths you've learned?

How have those truths stretched you or encouraged you to awaken to the Holy Spirit more?

After reviewing the five Scripture memory coloring pages, which Scripture stands out to you the most? Why?

What's one practical application from going through this study that you've put into practice?

How has the Holy Spirit prompted changes in your attitudes, actions, and behaviors because of this study?

What fruit has the Holy Spirit produced in your life because of this study?

The Holy Spirit often speaks in whispers and echoes—not to be secretive but to draw us closer and to invite us into deeper listening. In the quiet corners of your heart, what words has the Spirit been speaking specifically to you? Write or draw them in the space below.

PERSONAL STUDY CATCH-UP DAYS 4 & 5

HOLY SPIRIT, I TRUST YOU

Use these extra days to go back and complete any of the reflection questions or activities from the previous days week that you were unable to finish.

OPTIONAL:

Spend the two days reading through and completing *The God You Need to Know* book.

Whenever you aren't sure what the Holy Spirit is saying to you, remember this: The Spirit's native language is always love. Every nudge, every correction, every insight will ultimately lead you deeper into love—for God, for others, and even for yourself, so you become a greater conduit of God's relentless love everywhere you go.

Thank you for making this journey with me. Thank you for taking time to remember that the Spirit has been here since the beginning, since the curtain rose on the dawn of time.

"In the beginning, God . . ."

That's where we discover the God who speaks, the Jesus who creates, and the Spirit who hovers over our *tohu wa vohu* and moves in our mayhem. The Spirit who uses what we make to make a difference and wears us like a garment. The Spirit who sometimes works in stages and can breathe life into the darkest of nights, the most barren of places, and the bleakest of situations. The Spirit who says, "Go" and remains by our side.

Truly, this is the God we need to embrace and understand. This is the God we need to know.

With all my love,

♡ Margaret ♡

PS: If the Spirit revealed something meaningful to you through this study, would you kindly let me know at **hello@margaretfeinberg.com**? It would make my day.

LEADER'S GUIDE

If you are reading this, you have likely agreed to lead a group through *The God You Need to Know*. I am so proud of you! Thank you for loving those around you enough to be willing to serve them in this way. I have a hunch the Spirit will bless you in the weeks to come.

The God You Need to Know is a six-session study built around video-teaching content and small-group interaction. As the group leader, imagine yourself as the host of a lovely dinner party . . . without dinner, unless you love serving food like I do. Your job is to care for your "guests" so that as they arrive, they feel comfortable, welcome, and excited to learn straight away.

As the group leader, you are more of a facilitator than a teacher. Your role is not to answer all the questions or reteach the content—the video, book, and study guide will do most of that work. Your job is to guide the experience and cultivate your small group into a learning and growing community. This will make it a place for members to process, question, reflect, and grow together.

There are several elements in this leader's guide that will help you as you structure your study and reflection time, so follow along and take advantage of each one.

BEFORE YOU BEGIN

Materials

Before your first meeting, make sure the participants have a copy of this study guide. Alternately, you can hand out the study guides at your first meeting and give the group members some time to look over the material and ask any preliminary questions. During your first meeting, be sure to send a sheet around the room and have the members write down their names, phone numbers, and email addresses so you can keep in touch with them during the week.

Free Streaming Video Access

Additionally, spend a few minutes going over how to access the FREE streaming videos using the code printed on the inside front cover of each study guide. Helping everyone understand how accessible this material is will go a long way if anyone (including you) has to miss a meeting or if any member of your group chooses to lead a study after the conclusion of this one.

A few commonly-asked questions and answers:

Do I have to subscribe to StudyGateway? No. If you sign up for StudyGateway for the first time using studygateway.com/redeem you will not be prompted to subscribe, then or after.

Do I set up another account if I do another study later? No. The next time you do a HarperChristian Resources study with FREE streaming access, all you need to do is enter the new access code and the videos will be added to your account library.

There is a short video available that walks you through how to access your streaming video library. You can choose to show the video at your first meeting, or simply direct your group to the HarperChristian Resources YouTube channel to watch it at their convenience.

HOW TO ACCESS FREE STREAMING VIDEOS: https://youtu.be/JPhG06ksOn8

Group Size

Generally, the ideal size for a group is eight to ten people, which ensures everyone will have enough time to participate in discussions. If you have more people, you might want to break up the main group into smaller subgroups. Encourage those who show up at the first meeting to commit to attending the duration of the study, as this will help the group members get to know each other, create stability for the group, and help you know how to prepare each week.

Opening

At the beginning of each session welcome everyone, invite a participant to pray for the time together, and if it fits within your group's timeframe, consider discussing the opening questions or engaging in the opening activity (Session 3 and Session 6).

When prompted to select a volunteer to read a passage of any sort, please take the temperature of the room, as it were. Note the members of your group who do not readily raise their hands to volunteer. Reading Scripture aloud can incite anxiety or nervousness in some people. Please take the time in Session 1 to communicate the value of reading Scripture aloud in community. Encourage all your group members to try it at some point. Be clear that there is no bad reading of God's Word; rather it is meant to be read and shared with others. So, everyone should consider your group space a safe place to try to grow in this practice. One goal of this study is to grow participants in their overall engagement of God's Word, which includes feeling comfortable and confident with the words on the pages.

Preparing Your Group for the Study

Before watching your first video at your first meeting, let the group members know that each session contains five days' worth of Bible study and reflection materials to complete during the week between group meetings. While the personal study is optional, it will help the members cement the concepts presented during the group study time, dive deeper into the content, and encourage them to spend time each day in God's Word. It is my prayer and hope that you and your group will find joy and anticipation in reading God's Word and growing in relationship with the Holy Spirit during this study.

Also, invite your group members to bring any questions and insights they uncovered while reading to your next meeting, especially if they had a breakthrough moment or if they didn't understand something.

WEEKLY PREPARATION

As the leader, there are a few things you should do to prepare for each meeting:

- **Watch the video.** This will help you to become familiar with the content that's being presented and give you insight into what may or may not be brought up in the discussion time.
- **Read through the group discussion section.** This will help you to become familiar with the questions you will be asking, the focus Scripture, and the context. This practice allows you to better anticipate any alterations you might need or want to make in the discussion time for your best group experience.
- **Decide which questions you definitely want to discuss.** Based on the amount of questions and the length of group discussion, you may not be able to get through all the questions, so pre-select four to five questions that you definitely want to cover.
- **Be familiar with the questions you want to discuss.** Every group has times when there are no respondents and the question falls flat out of the gate. This is normal and okay. Be prepared with YOUR answer to the questions so you can always offer to share as an icebreaker and example, but try to be the last to answer, rather than the first. What you want to avoid is always answering the questions and impeding the discussion rather than helping it flourish. Foremost, encourage members of the group to answer questions.
- **Remind your group there are no wrong answers or dumb questions.** Note that in most cases there will not be one "right" answer to the question. Answers will vary, especially when the group members are being asked to share their personal experiences and stories.
- **Pray for your group.** Pray for your group members throughout the week and ask God to lead them as they study his Word.
- **Bring extra supplies to your meeting.** The members should bring their own

pens for writing notes, but it's a good idea to have extras available for those who forget. You may also want to bring paper and additional Bibles. If you find group members who are without a personal copy of the Bible, please let me know. There are a lot of great resources for low-cost outreach Bibles. I do not want anyone to be without a copy of the Bible if I can help it.

STRUCTURING THE DISCUSSION TIME

You will need to determine with your group how long you want to meet each week so you can plan your time accordingly. Generally, most groups like to meet for either sixty minutes or ninety minutes, so you could use one of the following schedules:

Section	60 min	90 min
WELCOME AND PRAYER (members arrive and get settled; leader reads or summarizes introduction)	1–5 minutes	1–5 minutes
OPENING GROUP DISCUSSION / ACTIVITY	5–10 minutes	5–10 minutes
WATCH VIDEO (watch the teaching video together and take notes)	5–10 minutes	5–10 minutes
GROUP DISCUSSION (discuss the Bible study questions you selected ahead of time)	20–30 minutes	50–60 minutes
CLOSING PRAYER (pray together as a group and dismiss)	1–5 minutes	1–5 minutes

As the group leader, it is up to you to keep track of the time and keep things moving along according to your schedule. You might want to set a timer for each segment so both you and the group members know when your time is up. (Note that there are some good phone apps for timers that play a gentle chime or other pleasant sound instead of a disruptive noise.)

Don't be concerned if the group members are quiet or slow to share. People are often quiet when they are pulling together their ideas, and this might be a new experience for them. Just ask a question and let it hang in the air until someone shares. You can then say, "Thank you. What about others? What came to you when you watched that portion of the video?"

GROUP DYNAMICS

Leading a group through *The God You Need to Know* will prove to be highly rewarding both to you and your group members. However, this doesn't mean you will not encounter any challenges along the way. Discussions can get off track. Group members may not be sensitive to the needs and ideas of others. Some might worry they will be expected to talk about matters that make them feel awkward. Others may express comments that result in disagreements. To help ease this strain on you and the group, consider the following ground rules:

- When someone raises a question or comment that is off the main topic, suggest you deal with it another time, or, if you feel led to go in that direction, let the group know you will be spending some time discussing it.
- If someone asks a question you don't know how to answer, admit it and move on. At your discretion, feel free to invite group members to comment on questions that call for personal experience.
- If you find one or two people are dominating the discussion time, direct a few questions to others in the group. Outside the main group time, ask the more dominating members to help you draw out the quieter ones. Work to make them a part of the solution instead of the problem.

- When a disagreement occurs, encourage the group members to process the matter in love. Encourage those on opposite sides to restate what they heard the other side say about the matter, and then invite each side to evaluate if that perception is accurate. Lead the group in examining other scriptures related to the topic and look for common ground.

When any of these issues arise, encourage your group members to follow these words from the Bible: "Love one another" (John 13:34), "If it is possible, as far as it depends on you, live at peace with everyone" (Romans 12:18), and "Be quick to listen, slow to speak and slow to become angry" (James 1:19). This will make your group time more rewarding and beneficial for everyone who attends.

SESSION-BY-SESSION OVERVIEWS

01 **Session 1: In Step with the Spirit**

Description: This session asks participants to consider that Acts 2 and Pentecost are not the Holy Spirit's grand debut; rather, they're a culmination of the Spirit's presence and power since the beginning of time.

Scripture covered in this session: Genesis 1:2; Psalm 51:10–11; Judges 15:14; Acts 2:1–18

Scripture Memory: Luke 11:13

Scripture during personal study days: Acts 1:8; 2:38; John 1:1–5, 9–13; 14:1, 16, 25–26; 16:13–15; Romans 5:3–5; 8:10–11, 14–16, 26; Luke 11:13; 1 Corinthians 2:13; 3:16, 18; 2 Corinthians 3:18; Genesis 1:2; 1 Thessalonians 1:5; 2 Thessalonians 2:13; Jude 1:20–21; Colossians 1:15–16

Discussion Question choices / notes:
_____
_____
_____
_____
_____

Prayer requests:
_____
_____
_____
_____
_____

02 Session 2: The Spirit Who Hovers

Description: This session reveals that since the opening of Genesis, the Spirit appears, not as a momentary flash, but as one who hovers over the uncertainty and unknown in our cosmos and our personal lives. This reminds us that no matter what we're facing, chaos does not have the final say.

Scripture covered in this session: Genesis 1:1–2; Deuteronomy 32:10–11; Luke 13:34; Psalm 139:7–16

Scripture Memory: Genesis 1:1–2

Scripture during personal study days: Job 27:3–4; Genesis 2:7; 37:5–9; 41:14–33; Ecclesiastes 12:7; John 3:7–8; 14:26; 20:21–22; Luke 10:21; 24:32; 1 Thessalonians 1:4–5; Romans 15:13; Acts 2:17, 37–38; 4:31; 9:31; 13:2–4; Ephesians 4:2–3; Judges 14:6; Ezekiel 3:14–15; 8:3; 36:26–27; Isaiah 61:1–3; 11:2; 1 Corinthians 2:10–12; Psalm 45:1

Discussion Question choices / notes:

_____
_____
_____
_____
_____

Prayer requests:

_____
_____
_____
_____
_____

03 Session 3: The Spirit Who Makes

Description: This session examines how the same Spirit who empowered Bezalel, Oholiab, and their guild of artisans, empowers us to be makers who display the glory of God.

Scripture covered in this session: Exodus 31:1–7; 35:34; 38:23; Psalm 90:17

Scripture Memory: Exodus 31:1–4

Scripture during personal study days: Proverbs 3:19–20; 9:10; Colossians 1:9–12; Acts 2:42–47; Numbers 11:10–17, 24–29; Ephesians 3:16–19; Daniel 1:4, 12–13, 17, 20; 4:8–9, 18; 5:9–12, 14; 6:1–4, 10; 10:2–3 (or Daniel chapters 1–6; 10); Exodus 31:3

Discussion Question choices / notes:
_____
_____
_____
_____
_____

Prayer requests:
_____
_____
_____
_____
_____
_____

04 Session 4: The Beauty of Discernment

Description: This session explores how just like David and Gideon we need markers for recognizing and discerning the Spirit's presence and prompting in our lives. It offers five practical guardrail questions for the discernment process.

Scripture covered in this session: Judges 6:12–24, 33–34; 1 Samuel 16:13; 2 Samuel 23:1–2; Matthew 23:34

Scripture Memory: Galatians 5:22–23

Scripture during personal study days: Judges 6:36–40; Genesis 24:12–19; 1 Samuel 14:6–12; Luke 1:5–20, 62–66; Matthew 14:22–29; 18:20; 22:37–40; John 15:13; 17:17; 20:24–29; Acts 1:21–26; Psalm 119:105; Hebrews 4:12; Deuteronomy 6:4–6; Galatians 5:22–23; Philippians 4:7; Ecclesiastes 4:9; Proverbs 27:17; James 5:16; Proverbs 12:18; Job 12:10; 32:1–14, 17–19; 33:4; 1 Corinthians 13:1–3

Discussion Question choices / notes:

_____
_____
_____
_____
_____

Prayer requests:

_____
_____
_____
_____
_____
_____

05 Session 5: The Spirit's Delightful Surprises

Description: This session looks to Ezekiel and how the Spirit of the Living God works through divine sequences and timetables, carefully and purposefully bringing about new life over time. It examines how the Spirit sometimes surprises and delights us in the most wonderful ways.

Scripture covered in this session: Ezekiel 2:1–8; 37:3–10; Romans 8:11

Scripture Memory: Ezekiel 37:5–6

Scripture during personal study days: 1 Kings 19:1–18; Genesis 39:20–23; 41:38–41; Judges 3:7–11; Luke 2:25–35; Romans 14:17

Discussion Question choices / notes:

Prayer requests:

06 **Session 6: When the Spirit Says "Go!"**

Description: This final session weaves together the lessons from throughout the study to reveal how the Spirit works throughout the Old Testament. We arrive at Acts 2 and Pentecost and can't help but think, *Of course, it would happen this way!* It challenges participants to practice small obedience whenever the Spirit says "Go!" and live in holy awe of what might unfold.

Scripture covered in this session: Acts 2:1–11, 38–41

Scripture Memory: Acts 2:38–39

Scripture during personal study days: Judges 4:4–9; Isaiah 6:1–9; Jeremiah 1:4–10; Amos 7:12–15; Matthew 28:19–20; Acts 8:26–40

Discussion Question choices / notes:

_____
_____
_____
_____
_____
_____

Prayer requests:

_____
_____
_____
_____
_____
_____
_____

NOTES

1. Jack Levison, *40 Days with the Holy Spirit* (Paraclete, 2015), 5–6.

2. Walter C. Kaiser Jr., "The Pentateuch," in *A Biblical Theology of the Holy Spirit*, ed. Trevor J. Burke and Keith Warrington (Cascade, 2014), 5–6.

3. Henry and Richard Blackaby with Claude King, *Experiencing God: Knowing and Doing the Will of God*, rev. ed. (B&H Publishing Group, 2008).

4. Jack Levison, *Inspired: The Holy Spirit and the Mind of Faith* (Eerdmans, 2013), 32–36.

5. Jack Levison, *A Boundless God: The Spirit According to the Old Testament* (Baker Academic, 2020), 167.

MEET MARGARET

Margaret Feinberg is a radiant soul whose infectious laughter and boundless enthusiasm have earned her a reputation as someone who doesn't just teach about joy—she embodies it.

Growing up with an artist's heart, a storyteller's mind, and a journalist's curiosity, Margaret has spent most of her life inspiring others to live with wide-eyed faith, unbridled joy, and a deep sense of wonder when it comes to God and Scripture.

Because, as she so often reminds us, God's presence is all around—if we'll just pause long enough to delight in the One who delights in us.

Host of the podcast, The Joycast, Margaret is a Bible teacher and speaker at churches and leading conferences. Her books and Bible studies, including Scouting the Divine, Fight Back With Joy, Taste and See, and Revelation: Extravagant Hope, have sold well over a million copies and received critical acclaim and extensive media coverage from USA Today, Los Angeles Times, Washington Post, and more. She was even named one of 50 women most shaping culture and the church today by Christianity Today.

When she's not writing or speaking at gatherings across the globe, you'll likely find Margaret making creative messes throughout the house, swimming like a dolphin at her local pool, or laughing around the table with friends, her husband, Leif, and their forever puppy, Zoom.

Margaret loves connecting with readers online and through speaking at live events. Whether you have a heartfelt or whimsy message to send or you're planning an event, she'd love to connect!

Feel free to drop her a note at hello@margaretfeinberg.com.

YOU CAN AWAKEN TO THE HOLY SPIRIT LIKE NEVER BEFORE

Available in stores and online!

OTHER BIBLE STUDIES BY MARGARET

We are made to experience and express God's love and beauty.

Both Genesis and the Gospel of John are written to spark your desire to pursue a deeper relationship with Jesus Christ. In this twelve-session video Bible study, you will reflect deeply on your relationship with God and awaken to the Lord's infinite beauty and love in a fresh and transformative way.

Take a delectable pilgrimage to discover the secret to savoring every day.

Join Margaret in this deeply nourishing six week video Bible study sprinkled with delicious recipes and tangible insights. After all, it's at the table where we learn to taste and see the goodness of God!

OTHER BIBLE STUDIES BY MARGARET

What if God's Final Word is Really a Rescue Plan?

In this six-session video Bible study Margaret will share how through the book of Revelation, God is saving the best for last! A survival guide, book of promises, and a banner of hope, Revelation is a love letter for the church for all time

How Much is Your Faith Making a Difference in Your Life?

Join Margaret in this rich, fresh study of James that will uncover the genuine markers of real faith, equip you to break free from old patterns by developing new practices, and discover how God treasures you.

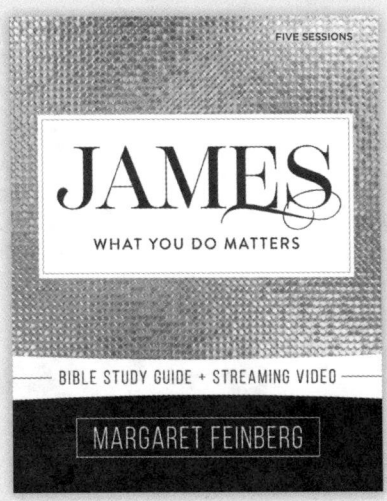

One of Margaret's greatest joys is speaking to live audiences. If you have a gathering of 250 or more, consider her for your next event.

Simply email:
booking@margaretfeinberg.com
for more details.